MICHAEL DRAYTON

selected poems

edited by
Vivien Thomas

Fyfield Books
Carcanet · Manchester

SBN 85635 225 X—cloth
SBN 85635 226 8—paper

First published 1977 by
Carcanet New Press Limited
330 Corn Exchange
Manchester M4 3BG

Printed in Great Britain by
W. & J. Mackay Ltd., Chatham

£4-95

MICHAEL DRAYTON

CONTENTS

INTRODUCTION

MICHAEL DRAYTON is a remarkably versatile poet. His career spans four decades and reflects many changes in poetic fashion; yet there is a stubborn independence and a continuity in all his work. He was committed to the high Renaissance ideal of the poet's calling and was always faithful to the tradition he inherited from Sidney and Spenser. Drayton himself tells us that his closest literary friendships were with William Browne, Sir William Alexander and William Drummond of Hawthornden; tradition also associates him with Jonson and Shakespeare.

His career is like that of Shakespeare in some ways. Both men were born in Warwickshire: Drayton in 1563, Shakespeare in the following year. Both came to London where they made names for themselves by writing. Both, although of yeoman stock, acquired coats of arms; Drayton's, appropriately, are 'a Pegasus salient argent'. Both wrote for the stage, but Drayton did so only for a short period. Between 1597 and 1602 he had a hand in some twenty-five plays, of which only one survives, the First Part of *Sir John Oldcastle*, 1599, written in collaboration with Richard Hathway, Anthony Munday and Robert Wilson.

Drayton began and ended his career with religious poetry, and his first publication in 1591 was a set of Biblical paraphrases. His later religious poetry takes the form of sacred epic. Although a religious man, however, he was not a great religious poet, and in *David and Goliath* and *Noah's Flood*, 1630, it is the opportunities for description (the entry of the animals into the ark, for example) that take hold of the poet's imagination, rather than the strictly religious aspects of his theme. His first important publication was a pastoral poem, *The Shepherd's Garland*, 1593, which is closely modelled on Spenser's *The Shepheardes Calendar*, 1579. As in Spenser we find a song in praise of Queen Elizabeth and a lament for Sir Philip Sidney's death; a shepherd (Rowland), who like Spenser's Colin represents the poet and is suffering from unrequited love; and the frequent use of dialect and archaic words. Drayton's poem, however, is not merely derivative. The song to Queen Elizabeth rivals Spenser's and the delightful burlesque ballad of Dowsabel has no precise analogue in Spenser.

In 1606, Drayton published a revised version of the work under the title of *Pastorals*. A new confidence in his own powers is everywhere apparent here. In his preface he defers to Spenser as 'the prime pastoralist of England', but affirms that his own pastorals are 'bold upon a new strain' and 'must speak for themselves'. The archaisms and dialect words have largely disappeared. A new eclogue, the ninth, has been added, in which the life of rural England, only occasionally glimpsed in the original eclogues, blends perfectly with the artificiality of pastoral. In his later pastoral poetry, there is a contrast between 'the hateful world' and the earthly paradise. In *The Muses' Elizium*, 1630, Elizium is the ideal world of the poet's imagination and Felicia the world of harsh reality. The old satyr from Felicia who finds a refuge in Elizium is a spokesman for Drayton himself, who found much that was uncongenial in the age into which he had survived. This enchanting poem is a new kind of pastoral, peopled by nymphs, swains and fairies, in which the traditional shepherd has only a minor place. It was written when Drayton was sixty-seven, in the year before his death in 1631, and is an astonishing example of his capacity for growth and change.

In *The Muses' Elizium* the follies of Felicia are viewed with a serene detachment. The satires, by contrast, are indignant in feeling and, in accordance with the literary theory of the time, often aggressively 'low' in style. *The Owl*, 1604, is a denunciation of corruption and vice, aimed initially at the court of Elizabeth, and masked in the politic obscurity of a bird-fable. The sharp-eyed owl reveals the abuses he has witnessed at court to the eagle, in whom James I is hinted at. Drayton was never favoured at James's court and his failure to receive recognition there continually rankled with him. In *The Mooncalf*, 1627, the creature of the title represents the monstrous new age and its birth is the occasion for a vigorous attack on luxury, effeminacy in men, masculinity in women, and the neglect of the arts.

Satire also contributes to the elegies, the sonnets, and the narrative poem *The Man in the Moon*, 1606. The last of these is a revision of *Endymion and Phoebe*, 1595, in which Drayton followed the fashion for Ovidian romance set by Marlowe's *Hero and Leander*, *c.* 1591, and Shakespeare's *Venus and Adonis*, 1593. Drayton's version is different from either of its predecessors in that it reconciles sensuous

8

delights with morality and Platonic idealism. Phoebe disguises herself as a nymph in order to woo the reluctant Endymion and then reveals that she is the goddess he has always worshipped. This appears to be Drayton's own variation on the legend. In *The Man in the Moon*, the luxuriant descriptions of ideal beauty have been drastically cut and the story of the nymph has disappeared. In their place are realistic descriptions and satire. The changes bring the poem into line with the new Jacobean literary fashion, but are a poor substitute for the original, which was never reprinted in Drayton's lifetime.

Comparable changes, but much more complex and rewarding ones, may be observed in the long and involved history of Drayton's sonnet sequence. This was first published under the title of *Idea's Mirror* in 1594, at the height of the popularity of the sonnet sequence celebrating the poet's love for his idealized mistress. Drayton's model was Samuel Daniel's *Delia*, 1591-2, and like Daniel's his theme is unrequited love patiently endured. His style frequently lacks Daniel's clarity and restraint, yet it is capable of an energy of imagination beyond Daniel's range, as in 'My heart imprisoned in a hopeless isle'. In 1599 the original sequence of fifty-one sonnets was fundamentally changed by the omission of twenty-one sonnets and the addition of twenty-eight new ones. The new sonnets are very different from their predecessors. They are influenced by Sidney's *Astrophil and Stella*, 1591, and like many of Sidney's sonnets, they are dramatic rather than lyrical, and playful, self-mocking and ironic in tone. Realism and topical reference give scope for individuality and bring love into relation with other concerns. The reader is warned that 'in all humours sportively I range'; the lady is teased, admonished and even addressed as 'an evil spirit'. On at least two occasions Drayton rejected a sonnet worth keeping, but in general his judgement was sound. The revised sequence shows an increased awareness both of the nature of love and of the possibilities of the sonnet form.

The process of revision did not stop after 1599, although none of the later revisions was so extensive. Four more editions of the sonnets appeared, in 1600, 1602, 1605 and 1619. On each occasion more sonnets were added and more of the original sonnets discarded, as well as some of the 1599 additions. The sonnets added in 1605 introduce a gravely meditative note into the sequence and are the most personal that Drayton had yet written. By 1619 the vogue for sonnets had long passed, but Drayton was never a mere follower of fashion and his interest in the form was undiminished. For the 1619 edition of his poems he wrote another ten sonnets, which are charged with renewed satirical energy and include the well-known 'Since there's no help, come let us kiss and part'. The final sequence consists of sixty-three sonnets, of which only twenty date from 1594.

'Idea' is Drayton's name for Anne Goodere, the younger daughter of Sir Henry Goodere, Drayton's first patron, in whose household he was brought up as a page. In 1595 or 1596 Anne married Henry Rainsford. Drayton never married, nor is there evidence to connect him romantically with any woman other than Anne. His sonnet sequence, in its later forms, is remarkable for its variety; it lacks consistent theme and narrative progression, nor can it be related in any form to the real state of affairs between Drayton and Anne Goodere. He does seem to have felt a life-long affection for her and for her husband and often stayed with them at their home at Clifford Chambers, 'which many a time hath been the muse's quiet port'. The nature of the sequence, however, was determined by literary convention and by the course of Drayton's poetic development, of which it is a fascinating record.

The historical narrative poem was another fashion of the 1590s that Drayton made his own and at which he worked with dogged persistence for many years. He began with the Legends, i.e. first-person narrative, as exemplified by Daniel's popular and influential *Complaint of Rosamund*, 1592. Drayton's subjects are Piers Gaveston, the favourite of Edward II; Matilda Fitzwalter, the chaste object of King John's amorous advances; and Robert of Normandy, the eldest son of William the Conqueror. Published between 1593 and 1596, all these poems are romantic and heavily decorated and diffuse in style. Like the early sonnets they underwent a detailed revision, in their case for the first collected edition of Drayton's poems in 1605. In 1607 they were joined by *The Legend of Cromwell*, which is written in the later, more sober and condensed style and shows a more factual and critical approach to history than do the earlier poems. This is also true of *The Barons' Wars*, 1603, which is a revision of *Mortimeriados*, 1596. The change of title is appropriate, since the role of Mortimer is not as central in the revised version as in the

10

original. In the second version the emphasis is on 'the bloody factions and rebellious pride' of Edward II's barons. The revision is the most thoroughgoing that even Drayton ever undertook; it includes introducing a number of new facts and recasting the poem into eight-line *ottava rima* stanzas instead of seven-line rhyme royal ones. Even so he was unsatisfied and in 1619 revised the poem yet again. This final stylistic revision sometimes shows an obsessive tendency to second thoughts, but in general the style of *The Barons' Wars* is a great improvement on that of *Mortimeriados*. Unnecessary epithets and excessive alliteration are omitted and the introduction of carefully balanced antitheses gives the style a new weight and precision.

In *England's Heroical Epistles*, Drayton at last found a form of his own for historical themes. He still has a model to follow, but in this case it is the *Heroides* ('Letters of the Heroines') of Ovid, a series of epistles supposed to have been written by legendary women. The theme is always love and the occasion for writing usually a moment of crisis; replies are usually not given. Drayton, as his title implies, transfers the method to English historical characters, and in his version every letter receives a reply, which greatly extends the dramatic possibilities of the form. The verse-form he uses is the closed couplet, adopted in imitation of Ovid's elegiac couplets (a hexameter followed by a pentameter), and handled in a manner that at times suggests the style of the English Augustan poets. The *Heroical Epistles* were the most popular of his poems with his contemporaries, running through five editions between 1597 and 1602, besides appearing in collected editions of Drayton's poems thereafter. Even Drayton must have thought them a success, since he never revised them very much.

In publishing a collection of odes in 1606 Drayton was for once making an innovation, not following a fashion, although he was to some extent indebted to the precedents of Du Bellay and Ronsard. In his preface he refers to the odes of Pindar, Horace and Anacreon, but, as he acknowledges, his own odes owe nothing to the first of these. The influence of Anacreon is evident, but slight; that of Horace is more pervasive, but Drayton's metres are derived not from the classics but principally from Ronsard, Skelton and Wyatt. The odes are a remarkably varied set of poems, in form and content. In 'The Heart' Drayton employs, unusually, the closely reasoned,

11

paradoxical style of the Metaphysicals; 'To His Rival' and 'To His Coy Love' have a new urbanity and ease that anticipate the lyrics of the Cavalier poets; in the vigorously patriotic 'To the Virginian Voyage' and the 'Ballad of Agincourt' he is eminently himself.

In *Elegies Upon Sundry Occasions*, 1627, Drayton once more took up an established form, but as usual his use of it was individual. In his time the word 'elegy' had a number of widely differing connotations. The verse-form used is generally the decasyllabic couplet (again, an approximation to the classical elegiac couplet); the poems themselves range from funeral elegies to verse-letters and from love poems to attacks on corruption. Drayton's elegies illustrate all these possibilities and his style varies from that of 'On His Lady's Not Coming to London', in which he pays bantering compliments in the Metaphysical manner, to the informal, prosaic style of the epistle to Henry Reynolds, in which he surveys the history of English poetry and delivers some shrewd critical opinions.

Drayton's longest poem, the 'topo-chronological' *Poly-Olbion*, was the result of the 'strange Herculean toil' of many years. A reference by Francis Meres tells us that Drayton was working on the poem as early as 1598. The first eighteen 'Songs' (published 1612) and the next twelve (published 1622) celebrate England and Wales. A further section on Scotland was planned but never completed, and nothing of it has survived. Drayton's heroic enterprise met with an unenthusiastic reception and he had difficulty in finding a publisher for his Second Part. Sadly, he had outlived his audience. *Poly-Olbion* is a spacious poem in ambling alexandrines, a poem to wander about in, like the country it celebrates. William Camden's *Britannia*, 1586-1607, is the principal source of the poem, but Drayton also writes from first-hand experience, gained from his extensive travels in England and Wales. His love of history, legend, antiquities and folk-lore is evident throughout; sheep-farming and agriculture, plants, animals and birds are enthusiastically described; active scenes, like those of hunting, hawking and coursing, fill the poem with movement and life. The 'long verses' of *Poly-Olbion* did not please Ben Jonson; of their nature they lack the beauty of form and expressiveness of Drayton's other poetry. Nevertheless, *Poly-Olbion* is Drayton's greatest and most characteristic work and a most impressive achievement.

A Note on the Text

The text of this selection is based on that of Drayton's *Poems*, 1619, but I have occasionally preferred an earlier reading. I have included a selection of the earlier readings of *The Barons' Wars* in the notes, to give the reader an idea of the way in which Drayton revised the poem. Spelling and punctuation have been modernized.

IDEA, THE SHEPHERD'S GARLAND, 1593

Song from the third eclogue

O thou fair silver Thames, O clearest crystal flood,
Beta alone the phoenix is of all thy watery brood,
The queen of virgins only she,
And thou the queen of floods shalt be:
Let all thy nymphs be joyful then to see this happy day;
Thy Beta now alone shall be the subject of my lay.

With dainty and delightsome strains of sweetest virelays,
Come, lovely shepherds, sit we down and chant our Beta's praise,
And let us sing so rare a verse,
Our Beta's praises to rehearse,   10
That little birds shall silent be, to hear poor shepherds sing,
And rivers backward bend their course, and flow unto the spring.

Range all thy swans, fair Thames, together on a rank,
And place them duly one by one, upon thy stately bank;
Then set together all a-good,
Recording to the silver flood,
And crave the tuneful nightingale to help you with her lay,
The ouzel and the throstlecock, chief music of our May.

O, see what troops of nymphs been sporting on the strands,
And they been blessed nymphs of peace, with olives in their hands.
How merrily the Muses sing,   21
That all the flowery meadows ring,
And Beta sits upon the bank, in purple and in pall,
And she the queen of muses is, and wears the coronal.

Trim up her golden tresses with Apollo's sacred tree;
O happy sight unto all those that love and honour thee,
The blessed angels have prepared,
A glorious crown for thy reward,
Not such a golden crown as haughty Caesar wears,
But such a glittering starry crown as Ariadne bears.   30

15

Make her a goodly chaplet of azured columbine,
And wreathe about her coronet with sweetest eglantine;
Bedeck our Beta all with lilies,
And the dainty daffadillies,
With roses damask, white, and red, and fairest flower-de-lice,
With cowslips of Jerusalem, and cloves of Paradise.

O thou fair torch of heaven, the day's most dearest light,
And thou bright shining Cynthia, the glory of the night,
You stars the eyes of heaven,
And thou the gliding leven, 40
And thou, O gorgeous Iris, with all strange colours dyed,
When she streams forth her rays, then dashed is all your pride.

See how the day stands still, admiring of her face,
And Time, lo! stretcheth forth her arms, thy Beta to embrace;
The sirens sing sweet lays,
The Tritons sound her praise;
Go pass on, Thames, and hie thee fast unto the ocean sea,
And let thy billows there proclaim thy Beta's holiday.

And water thou the blessed root of that green olive tree,
With whose sweet shadow all thy banks with peace preservèd be, 50
Laurel for poets and conquerors,
And myrtle for love's paramours,
That fame may be thy fruit, the boughs preserved by peace,
And let the mournful cypress die, now storms and tempests cease.

We'll strew the shore with pearl where Beta walks alone,
And we will pave her princely bower with richest Indian stone;
Perfume the air and make it sweet,
For such a goddess it is meet,
For if her eyes for purity contend with Titan's light,
No marvel then although they so do dazzle human sight. 60

Sound out your trumpets then, from London's stately towers,
To beat the stormy winds aback and calm the raging showers;
Set too the cornet and the flute,

The orpharion and the lute,
And tune the tabor and the pipe to the sweet violons,
And move the thunder in the air with loudest clarions.

Beta, long may thine altars smoke with yearly sacrifice,
And long thy sacred temples may their sabbaths solemnize,
Thy shepherds watch by day and night,
Thy maids attend the holy light,   70
And thy large empire stretch her arms from east unto the west,
And thou under thy feet mayst tread that foul seven-headed beast.

PASTORALS, 1606

Part of the ninth eclogue

Late 'twas in June, the fleece when fully grown,
In the full compass of the passèd year,
The season well by skilful shepherds known,
That them provide immediately to shear.

Their lambs late waxed so lusty and so strong,
That time did them their mothers' teats forbid,
And in the fields the common flocks among,
Eat of the same grass that the greater did.

When not a shepherd anything that could,
But greased his start-ups black as autumn's sloe,   10
And for the better credit of the wold,
In their fresh russets everyone doth go.

Who now a posy pins not in his cap?
And not a garland baldric-wise doth wear?
Some, of such flowers as to his hand doth hap,
Others, such as a secret meaning bear:

He from his lass him lavender hath sent,
Showing her love, and doth requital crave;

17

Him rosemary his sweetheart, whose intent
Is that he her should in remembrance have.

Roses, his youth and strong desire express;
Her sage, doth show his sovereignty in all;
The Julyflower declares his gentleness;
Thyme, truth; the pansy, heartsease maidens call.

In cotes such simples, simply in request,
Wherewith proud courts in greatness scorn to mell,
For country toys become the country best,
And please poor shepherds, and become them well.

When the new-washed flock from the river's side,
Coming as white as January's snow,
The ram with nosegays bears his horns in pride,
And no less brave the bell-wether doth go.

After their fair flocks in a lusty rout,
Came the gay swains with bagpipes strongly blown,
And busied though this solemn sport about,
Yet had each one an eye unto his own.

And by the ancient statutes of the field,
He that his flocks the earliest lamb should bring
(As it fell out then, Rowland's charge to yield),
Always for that year was the shepherds' king.

And soon preparing for the shepherds' board,
Upon a green that curiously was squared,
With country cates being plentifully stored,
And 'gainst their coming handsomely prepared:

New whig, with water from the clearest stream,
Green plums, and wildings, cherries chief of feast,
Fresh cheese, and dowsets, curds and clouted cream,
Spiced syllabubs, and cider of the best.

And to the same down solemnly they sit,
In the fresh shadow of their summer bowers,   50
With sundry sweets them every way to fit,
The neighb'ring vale despoilèd of her flowers.

And whilst together merry thus they make,
The sun to west a little 'gan to lean,
Which the late fervour soon again did slake,
When as the nymphs came forth upon the plain.

Here might you many a shepherdess have seen,
Of which no place, as Cotswold, such doth yield;
Some of it native, some for love, I ween,
Thither were come from many a fertile field.   60

There was the widow's daughter of the glen,
Dear Rosalind, that scarcely brooked compare,
The Moorland maiden, so admired of men,
Bright Goldylocks, and Phillida the fair,

Lettice and Parnell, pretty lovely peats,
Cusse of the fold, the virgin of the well,
Fair Ambry with the alabaster teats,
And more, whose names were here too long to tell;

Which now came forward following their sheep,
Their batt'ning flocks on grassy leas to hold,   70
Thereby from scathe and peril them to keep,
Till evening come that it were time to fold.

When now, at last, as liked the shepherds' king
(At whose command they all obedient were)
Was pointed who the roundelay should sing,
And who again the under-song should bear.

The first whereof he Batte doth bequeath,
A wittier wag on all the wold's not found,

Gorbo, the man that him should sing beneath,
Which his loud bag-pipe skilfully could sound. 80

Who amongst all the nymphs that were in sight,
Batte his dainty Daffodil there missed,
Which, to enquire of, doing all his might,
Him his companion kindly doth assist.

Batte.   Gorbo, as thou cam'st this way,
           By yonder little hill,
           Or as thou through the fields didst stray,
           Saw'st thou my Daffodil?

           She's in a frock of Lincoln green,
           Which colour likes her sight, 90
           And never hath her beauty seen,
           But through a veil of white.

           Than roses richer to behold,
           That trim up lovers' bowers,
           The pansy and the marigold,
           Though Phoebus' paramours.

Gorbo.   Thou well describ'st the daffodil,
           It is not full an hour,
           Since by the spring, near yonder hill,
           I saw that lovely flower. 100

Batte.   Yet my fair flower thou didst not meet,
           Nor news of her didst bring,
           And yet my Daffodil's more sweet,
           Than that by yonder spring.

Gorbo.   I saw a shepherd that doth keep,
           In yonder field of lilies,
           Was making (as he fed his sheep)
           A wreath of daffodillies.

Batte.	Yet, Gorbo, thou delud'st me still,	
	My flower thou didst not see,	110
	For, know, my pretty Daffodil	
	Is worn of none but me.	

Batte. Yet, Gorbo, thou delud'st me still,
      My flower thou didst not see,   110
      For, know, my pretty Daffodil
      Is worn of none but me.

      To show itself but near her seat,
      No lily is so bold,
      Except to shade her from the heat,
      Or keep her from the cold.

Gorbo. Through yonder vale as I did pass,
      Descending from the hill,
      I met a smirking bonny lass,
      They call her Daffodil;   120

      Whose presence, as along she went,
      The pretty flowers did greet,
      As though their heads they downward bent,
      With homage to her feet.

      And all the shepherds that were nigh,
      From top of every hill,
      Unto the valleys loud did cry,
      'There goes sweet Daffodil.'

Batte. Ay, gentle shepherd, now with joy
      Thou all my flocks dost fill;   130
      That's she alone, kind shepherd's boy,
      Let us to Daffodil.

SONNETS FROM *IDEA'S MIRROR* (1594) and *IDEA* (1599-1619)

1.

Clear Anker, on whose silver-sandèd shore,
My soul-shrined saint, my fair Idea lies,
O blessèd brook, whose milk-white swans adore
Thy crystal stream refinèd by her eyes,
Where sweet myrrh-breathing Zephyr in the spring,
Gently distils his nectar-dropping showers,
Where nightingales in Arden sit and sing,
Amongst the dainty dew-empearlèd flowers:
Say thus, fair brook, when thou shalt see thy queen,
'Lo, here thy shepherd spent his wand'ring years;
And in these shades, dear nymph, he oft hath been,
And here to thee he sacrificed his tears.'
Fair Arden, thou my Tempe art alone,
  And thou, sweet Anker, art my Helicon.   (1594-1619)

2.

The glorious sun went blushing to his bed,
When my soul's sun from her fair cabinet
Her golden beams had now discoverèd,
Light'ning the world, eclipsèd by his set.
Some mused to see the earth envy the air
Which from her lips exhaled refinèd sweet;
A world to see, yet how he joyed to hear
The dainty grass make music with her feet.
But my most marvel was when from the skies,
So comet-like each star advanced her light,
As though the heaven had now awaked her eyes,
And summoned angels to this blessed sight.
No cloud was seen, but crystalline the air,
  Laughing for joy upon my lovely fair.   (1594)

3.

My heart imprisoned in a hopeless isle,
Peopled with armies of pale jealous eyes,
The shores beset with thousand secret spies,
Must pass by air, or else die in exile.

22

He framed him wings with feathers of his thought,
Which by their nature learned to mount the sky,
And with the same he practisèd to fly,
Till he himself this eagle's art had taught.
Thus soaring still, not looking once below,
So near thine eyes' celestial sun aspired,
That with the rays his wafting pinions fired.
Thus was the wanton cause of his own woe.
Down fell he in thy beauty's ocean drenched,
Yet there he burns in fire that's never quenched.   (1594-1613)

4.

When first I ended, then I first began,
The more I travelled, further from my rest;
Where most I lost, there most of all I wan,
Pinèd with hunger, rising from a feast.
Methinks I fly, yet want I legs to go,
Wise in conceit, in act a very sot,
Ravished with joy amidst a hell of woe;
What most I seem, that surest am I not.
I build my hopes a world above the sky,
Yet with the mole I creep into the earth;
In plenty I am starved with penury,
And yet I surfeit in the greatest dearth.
I have, I want, despair, and yet desire,
Burned in a sea of ice, and drowned amidst a fire.   (1594-1619)

5.

Into these loves who but for passion looks,
At this first sight, here let him lay them by,
And seek elsewhere, in turning other books,
Which better may his labour satisfy.
No far-fetched sigh shall ever wound my breast;
Love from mine eye a tear shall never wring,
Nor in ah-mes my whining sonnets dressed;
A libertine, fantasticly I sing.
My verse is the true image of my mind,
Ever in motion, still desiring change;

And as thus to variety inclined,
So in all humours sportively I range.
My muse is rightly of the English strain,
That cannot long one fashion entertain. (1599-1619)

6.
My heart was slain, and none but you and I:
Who should I think the murder should commit?
Since, but yourself, there was no creature by,
But only I, guiltless of murd'ring it.
It slew itself; the verdict on the view
Do quit the dead, and me not accessary.
Well, well, I fear it will be proved by you;
The evidence so great a proof doth carry.
But O, see, see, we need enquire no further,
Upon your lips the scarlet drops are found,
And in your eye the boy that did the murder,
Your cheeks yet pale, since first he gave the wound.
By this I see, however things be passed,
Yet heav'n will still have murder out at last. (1599-1619)

7.
You not alone, when you are still alone,
O God, from you that I could private be!
Since you one were, I never since was one;
Since you in me, myself since out of me,
Transported from myself into your being;
Though either distant, present yet to either,
Senseless with too much joy, each other seeing,
And only absent when we are together.
Give me myself, and take yourself again,
Devise some means but how I may forsake you;
So much is mine that doth with you remain,
That taking what is mine, with me I take you.
You do bewitch me; O, that I could fly
From myself you, or from your own self I. (1599-1619)

8.

To nothing fitter can I thee compare,
Than to the son of some rich penny-father,
Who having now brought on his end with care,
Leaves to his son all he had heaped together.
This new-rich novice, lavish of his chest,
To one man gives, doth on another spend;
Then here he riots, yet amongst the rest,
Haps to lend some to one true honest friend.
Thy gifts thou in obscurity dost waste;
False friends thy kindness, born but to deceive thee,
Thy love, that is on the unworthy placed;
Time hath thy beauty, which with age will leave thee
Only that little which to me was lent,
I give thee back, when all the rest is spent.   (1599-1619)

9.

You cannot love, my pretty heart, and why?
There was a time you told me that you would,
But now again you will the same deny;
If it might please you, would to God you could.
What, will you hate? nay, that you will not neither;
Nor love, nor hate, how then? what will you do?
What, will you keep a mean then betwixt either?
Or will you love me, and yet hate me too?
Yet serves not this; what next, what other shift?
You will, and will not; what a coil is here!
I see your craft; now I perceive your drift,
And all this while, I was mistaken there:
Your love and hate is this—I now do prove you—
You love in hate, by hate to make me love you.   (1599-1619)

10.

An evil spirit, your beauty haunts me still,
Wherewith, alas, I have been long possessed,
Which ceaseth not to tempt me to each ill,
Nor gives me once but one poor minute's rest.
In me it speaks, whether I sleep or wake,

And when by means to drive it out I try,
With greater torments then it me doth take,
And tortures me in most extremity;
Before my face it lays down my despairs,
And hastes me on unto a sudden death,
Now tempting me to drown myself in tears,
And then in sighing to give up my breath.
Thus am I still provoked to every evil
By this good wicked spirit, sweet angel devil.   (1599-1619)

11.
Dear, why should you command me to my rest,
When now the night doth summon all to sleep?
Methinks this time becometh lovers best;
Night was ordained together friends to keep.
How happy are all other living things,
Which though the day disjoin by sev'ral flight,
The quiet evening yet together brings,
And each returns unto his love at night.
O, thou that art so courteous else to all!
Why shouldst thou, night, abuse me only thus,
That ev'ry creature to his kind dost call,
And yet 'tis thou dost only sever us?
Well could I wish it would be ever day,
If, when night comes, you bid me go away.   (1602-1619)

12.
Why should your fair eyes with such sov'reign grace
Disperse their rays on ev'ry vulgar spirit,
Whilst I in darkness, in the self-same place,
Get not one glance to recompense my merit?
So doth the ploughman gaze the wand'ring star,
And only rest contented with the light,
That never learned what constellations are,
Beyond the bent of his unknowing sight.
O, why should beauty (custom to obey)
To their gross sense apply herself so ill?
Would God I were as ignorant as they,

When I am made unhappy by my skill;
Only compelled on this poor good to boast,
Heav'ns are not kind to them that know them most.   (1605-1619)

13.
In pride of wit, when high desire of fame
Gave life and courage to my lab'ring pen,
And first the sound and virtue of my name
Won grace and credit in the ears of men,
With those the throngèd theatres that press,
I in the circuit for the laurel strove,
Where the full praise, I freely must confess,
In heat of blood, a modest mind might move.
With shouts and claps at ev'ry little pause,
When the proud round on ev'ry side hath rung,
Sadly I sit, unmoved with the applause,
As though to me it nothing did belong.
No public glory vainly I pursue;
All that I seek is to eternize you.   (1605-1619)

14.
Calling to mind since first my love begun,
Th'uncertain times oft varying in their course,
How things still unexpectedly have run,
As't please the fates, by their resistless force,
Lastly, mine eyes amazedly have seen
Essex' great fall, Tyrone his peace to gain,
The quiet end of that long-living queen,
This king's fair entrance, and our peace with Spain,
We and the Dutch at length ourselves to sever.
Thus the world doth, and evermore shall reel,
Yet to my goddess am I constant ever,
Howe'er blind fortune turn her giddy wheel.
Though heaven and earth prove both to me untrue,
Yet am I still inviolate to you.   (1605-1619)

15.
You, best discerned of my mind's inward eyes,
And yet your graces outwardly divine,

Whose dear remembrance in my bosom lies,
Too rich a relic for so poor a shrine,
You, in whom nature chose herself to view,
When she her own perfection would admire,
Bestowing all her excellence on you,
At whose pure eyes, love lights his hallowed fire;
Ev'n as a man that in some trance hath seen
More than his wond'ring utt'rance can unfold,
That rapt in spirit, in better worlds hath been,
So must your praise distractedly be told;
Most of all short, when I should show you most,
In your perfections so much am I lost.   (1605-1619)

16.
Like an adventurous seafarer am I,
Who hath some long and dang'rous voyage been,
And called to tell of his discovery,
How far he sailed, what countries he had seen,
Proceeding from the port whence he put forth,
Shows by his compass how his course he steered,
When east, when west, when south, and when by north,
As how the pole to ev'ry place was reared;
What capes he doubled, of what continent,
The gulfs and straits that strangely he had passed,
Where most becalmed, where with foul weather spent,
And on what rocks in peril to be cast.
Thus in my love, time calls me to relate
My tedious travels, and oft varying fate.   (1619)

17.
How many paltry, foolish, painted things,
That now in coaches trouble ev'ry street,
Shall be forgotten, whom no poet sings,
Ere they be well wrapped in their winding sheet?
Where I to thee eternity shall give,
When nothing else remaineth of these days,
And queens hereafter shall be glad to live
Upon the alms of thy superfluous praise;

Virgins and matrons, reading these my rhymes,
Shall be so much delighted with thy story,
That they shall grieve they lived not in these times,
To have seen thee, their sex's only glory.
So shalt thou fly above the vulgar throng,
Still to survive in my immortal song. (1619)

18.

Since to obtain thee nothing me will stead,
I have a med'cine that shall cure my love:
The powder of her heart dried, when she is dead,
That gold nor honour ne'er had power to move;
Mixed with her tears that ne'er her truelove crossed,
Nor at fifteen ne'er longed to be a bride,
Boiled with her sighs, in giving up the ghost,
That for her late deceasèd husband died;
Into the same then let a woman breathe
That, being chid, did never word reply,
With one thrice-married's prayers, that did bequeath
A legacy to stale virginity.
If this receipt have not the power to win me,
Little I'll say, but think the devil's in me. (1619)

19.

Since there's no help, come let us kiss and part:
Nay, I have done; you get no more of me,
And I am glad, yea, glad with all my heart,
That thus so cleanly I myself can free;
Shake hands for ever, cancel all our vows,
And when we meet at any time again,
Be it not seen in either of our brows,
That we one jot of former love retain.
Now at the last gasp of love's latest breath,
When, his pulse failing, passion speechless lies,
When faith is kneeling by his bed of death,
And innocence is closing up his eyes,
Now, if thou wouldst, when all have given him over,
From death to life thou mightst him yet recover. (1619)

ENDYMION AND PHOEBE, IDEA'S LATMUS, 1595

Lines 1-66

In Ionia whence sprang old poets' fame,
From whom that sea did first derive her name,
The blessèd bed whereon the Muses lay,
Beauty of Greece, the pride of Asia,
Whence Archelaus, whom times historify,
First unto Athens brought philosophy:
In this fair region on a goodly plain,
Stretching her bounds unto the bord'ring main,
The mountain Latmus overlooks the sea,
Smiling to see the ocean billows play: 10
Latmus, where young Endymion used to keep
His fairest flock of silver-fleecèd sheep.
To whom Silvanus often would resort
At barley-break to see the satyrs sport;
And when rude Pan his tabret list to sound,
To see the fair nymphs foot it in a round,
Under the trees which on this mountain grew,
As yet the like Arabia never knew;
For all the pleasures nature could devise
Within this plot she did imparadise,   20
And great Diana of her special grace
With vestal rites had hallowed all the place.
Upon this mount there stood a stately grove,
Whose reaching arms to clip the welkin strove,
Of tufted cedars, and the branching pine,
Whose bushy tops themselves do so entwine,
As seemed when nature first this work begun,
She then conspired against the piercing sun;
Under whose covert (thus divinely made)
Phoebus' green laurel flourished in the shade,   30
Fair Venus' myrtle, Mars his warlike fir,
Minerva's olive, and the weeping myrrh,
The patient palm, which thrives in spite of hate,
The poplar, to Alcides consecrate;

Which nature in such order had disposed,
And therewithal these goodly walks enclosed,
As served for hangings and rich tapestry,
To beautify this stately gallery.
Embroid'ring these in curious trails along,
The clustered grapes, the golden citrons hung;   40
More glorious than the precious fruit were these
Kept by the dragon in Hesperides,
Or gorgeous arras in rich colours wrought,
With silk from Afric, or from Indie brought.
Out of this soil sweet bubbling fountains crept,
As though for joy the senseless stones had wept;
With straying channels dancing sundry ways,
With often turns, like to a curious maze,
Which breaking forth, the tender grass bedewed,
Whose silver sand with orient pearl was strewed,   50
Shadowed with roses and sweet eglantine,
Dipping their sprays into this crystalline;
From which the birds the purple berries pruned,
And to their loves their small recorders tuned.
The nightingale, woods' herald of the spring,
The whistling ouzel, mavis caroling,
Tuning their trebles to the water's fall,
Which made the music more angelical,
Whilst gentle Zephyr murmuring among,
Kept time, and bare the burthen to the song.   60
About whose brims, refreshed with dainty showers,
Grew amaranthus and sweet gillyflowers,
The marigold, Phoebus' belovèd friend,
The moly, which from sorcery doth defend,
Violet, carnation, balm and cassia,
Idea's primrose, coronet of May.

The Epistle of Rosamond to King Henry II

If yet thine eyes, great Henry, may endure
These tainted lines, drawn with a hand impure,
Which fain would blush, but fear keeps blushes back,
And therefore suited in despairing black,
Let me for love's sake their acceptance crave—
But that sweet name vile I profanèd have;
Punish my fault, or pity mine estate,
Read them for love, if not for love, for hate.

    If with my shame thine eyes thou fain wouldst feed,
Here let them surfeit of my shame to read: 10
This scribbled paper which I send to thee,
If noted rightly, doth resemble me;
As this pure ground whereon these letters stand,
So pure was I, ere stainèd by thy hand;
Ere I was blotted with this foul offence,
So clear and spotless was mine innocence;
Now, like these marks which taint this hateful scroll,
Such the black sins which spot my leprous soul.

    What by this conquest canst thou hope to win,
Where thy best spoil is but the act of sin?   20
Why on my name this slander dost thou bring,
To make my fault renownèd by a king?
Fame never stoops to things but mean and poor,
The more our greatness, our fault is the more;
Lights on the ground themselves do lessen far,
But in the air each small spark seems a star.
Why on my woman-frailty shouldst thou lay
So strong a plot, mine honour to betray?
Or thy unlawful pleasure shouldst thou buy
Both with thine own shame, and my infamy?   30
'Twas not my mind consented to this ill—
Then had I been transported by my will;
For what my body was enforced to do,
Heaven knows my soul yet ne'er consented to;

For, through mine eyes had she her liking seen,
Such as my love, such had my lover been.
True love is simple, like his mother truth,
Kindly affection, youth to love with youth;
No greater corsive to our blooming years,
Than the cold badge of winter-blasted hairs. 40
Thy kingly power makes to withstand thy foes,
But cannot keep back age, with time it grows;
Though honour our ambitious sex doth please,
Yet in that honour, age a foul disease;
Nature hath her free course in all, and then
Age is alike, in kings and other men.
Which all the world will to my shame impute,
That I myself did basely prostitute,
And say that gold was fuel to the fire,
Grey hairs in youth not kindling green desire. 50
O no; that wicked woman, wrought by thee,
My tempter was to that forbidden tree;
That subtle serpent, that seducing devil,
Which bade me taste the fruit of good and evil;
That Circe, by whose magic I was charmed,
And to this monstrous shape am thus transformed;
That vip'rous hag, the foe to her own kind,
That devilish spirit, to damn the weaker mind;
Our frailty's plague, our sex's only curse,
Hell's deep'st damnation, the worst evil's worse. 60
   But Henry, how canst thou affect me thus,
T'whom thy remembrance now is odious?
My hapless name with Henry's name I found,
Cut in the glass with Henry's diamond;
That glass from thence fain would I take away,
But then I fear the air would me betray;
Then do I strive to wash it out with tears,
But then the same more evident appears.
Then do I cover it with my guilty hand,
Which that name's witness doth against me stand; 70
Once did I sin, which memory doth cherish;
Once I offended, but I ever perish.

What grief can be, but time doth make it less?
But infamy, time never can suppress.
Sometimes, to pass the tedious irksome hours,
I climb the top of Woodstock's mounting towers,
Where in a turret secretly I lie,
To view from far such as do travel by;
Whither, methinks, all cast their eyes at me,
As through the stones my shame did make them see,   80
And with such hate the harmless walls do view,
As ev'n to death their eyes would me pursue.
The married women curse my hateful life,
Wronging a fair queen and a virtuous wife;
The maidens wish I buried quick may die,
And from each place near my abode do fly.
Well knew'st thou what a monster I would be,
When thou didst build this labyrinth for me,
Whose strange meanders turning ev'ry way,
Be like the course wherein my youth did stray;   90
Only a clue doth guide me out and in,
But yet still walk I circular in sin.
    As in the gallery this other day,
I and my woman passed the time away,
'Mongst many pictures which were hanging by
The silly girl at length happed to espy
Chaste Lucrece' image, and desires to know,
What she should be, herself that murdered so?
'Why, girl,' quoth I, 'this is that Roman dame—'
Not able then to tell the rest for shame,   100
My tongue doth mine own guiltiness betray;
With that I sent the prattling wench away,
Lest when my lisping guilty tongue should halt,
My looks might prove the index to my fault.
As that life-blood which from the heart is sent,
In beauty's field pitching his crimson tent,
In lovely sanguine suits the lily cheek,
Whilst it but for a resting place doth seek;
And changing oftentimes with sweet delight,
Converts the white to red, the red to white;   110

The blush with paleness for the place doth strive,
The paleness thence the blush would gladly drive:
Thus in my breast a thousand thoughts I carry,
Which in my passion diversely do vary.
    When as the sun hales tow'rds the western slade,
And the trees' shadows hath much taller made,
Forth go I to a little current near,
Which like a wanton trail creeps here and there,
Where, with mine angle casting in my bait,
The little fishes (dreading the deceit) 120
With fearful nibbling fly th'enticing gin,
By nature taught what danger lies therein.
Things reasonless thus warned by nature be,
Yet I devoured the bait was laid for me.
Thinking thereon, and breaking into groans,
The bubbling spring which trips upon the stones,
Chides me away, lest sitting but too nigh,
I should pollute that native purity.
Rose of the world, so doth import my name,
Shame of the world, my life hath made the same, 130
And to th'unchaste this name shall given be,
Of Rosamond, derived from sin and me.
The Cliffords take from me that name of theirs,
Which hath been famous for so many years;
They blot my birth with hateful bastardy,
That I sprang not from their nobility;
They my alliance utterly refuse,
Nor will a strumpet shall their name abuse.
    Here in the garden, wrought by curious hands,
Naked Diana in the fountain stands, 140
With all her nymphs got round about to hide her,
As when Actaeon had by chance espied her:
This sacred image I no sooner viewed,
But as that metamorphosed man pursued
By his own hounds, so by my thoughts am I,
Which chase me still, which way soe'er I fly.
Touching the grass, the honey-dropping dew,
Which falls in tears before my limber shoe,

Upon my foot consumes in weeping still,
As it would say, 'Why went'st thou to this ill?'   150
Thus, to no place in safety can I go,
But everything doth give me cause of woe.
    In that fair casket, of such wondrous cost,
Thou sent'st the night before mine honour lost,
Amymone was wrought, a harmless maid,
By Neptune, that adult'rous god, betrayed;
She prostrate at his feet, begging with prayers,
Wringing her hands, her eyes swoll'n up with tears.
This was not an entrapping bait from thee,
But by thy virtue gently warning me,   160
And to declare for what intent it came,
Lest I therein should ever keep my shame.
And in this casket (ill I see it now)
That Jove's love Io, turned into a cow;
Yet was she kept with Argus' hundred eyes,
So wakeful still be Juno's jealousies.
By this I well might have forwarnèd been,
T'have cleared myself to thy suspecting queen,
Who with more hundred eyes attendeth me,
Than had poor Argus single eyes to see.   170
In this thou rightly imitatest Jove,
Into a beast thou hast transformed thy love;
Nay, worser far (beyond their beastly kind),
A monster both in body and in mind.
    The waxen taper which I burn by night,
With the dull vap'ry dimness mocks my sight,
As though the damp which hinders the clear flame,
Came from my breath, in that night of my shame;
When as it looked with a dark lowering eye,
To see the loss of my virginity.   180
And if a star but by the glass appear,
I straight entreat it not to look in here;
I am already hateful to the light,
And will it too betray me to the night?
    Then sith my shame so much belongs to thee,
Rid me of that, by only murd'ring me;

And let it justly to my charge be laid,
That I thy person meant to have betrayed;
Thou shalt not need by circumstance t'accuse me,
If I deny it, let the heavens refuse me.   190
My life's a blemish, which doth cloud thy name;
Take it away, and clear shall shine thy fame:
Yield to my suit, if ever pity moved thee;
In this show mercy, as I ever loved thee.

Henry to Rosamond

When first the post arrivèd at my tent,
And brought the letters Rosamond had sent,
Think from his lips but what dear comfort came,
When in mine ear he softly breathed thy name:
Straight I enjoined him of thy health to tell,
Longing to hear my Rosamond did well;
With new enquiries then I cut him short,
When of the same he gladly would report,
That with the earnest haste my tongue oft trips,
Catching the words half spoke out of his lips.   10
This told, yet more I urge him to reveal,
To lose no time, whilst I unripped the seal.
The more I read, still do I err the more,
As though mistaking somewhat said before:
Missing the point, the doubtful sense is broken,
Speaking again what I before had spoken.
Still in a swound, my heart revives and faints,
'Twixt hopes, despairs, 'twixt smiles and deep complaints.
As these sad accents sort in my desires,
Smooth calms, rough storms, sharp frosts, and raging fires,   20
Put on with boldness, and put back with fears,
For oft thy troubles do extort my tears.
O, how my heart at that black line did tremble,
That blotted paper should thyself resemble!
O, were there paper but near half so white!
The gods thereon their sacred laws would write

With pens of angels' wings; and for their ink,
That heavenly nectar, their immortal drink.
   Majestic courage strives to have suppressed
This fearful passion stirred up in my breast;   30
But still in vain the same I go about,
My heart must break within, or woes break out.
Am I at home pursued with private hate,
And war comes raging to my palace gate?
Is meagre envy stabbing at my throne,
Treason attending when I walk alone?
And am I branded with the curse of Rome,
And stand condemnèd by a council's doom?
And by the pride of my rebellious son,
Rich Normandy with armies over-run?   40
Fatal my birth, unfortunate my life,
Unkind my children, most unkind my wife.
Grief, cares, old age, suspicion to torment me,
Nothing on earth to quiet or content me;
So many woes, so many plagues to find,
Sickness of body, discontent of mind;
Hopes left, helps reft, life wronged, joy interdicted,
Banished, distressed, forsaken, and afflicted.
Of all relief hath fortune quite bereft me?
Only my love yet to my comfort left me: 50
And is one beauty thought so great a thing,
To mitigate the sorrows of a king?
Barred of that choice the vulgar often prove,
Have we, than they, less privilege in love?
Is it a king the woeful widow hears?
Is it a king dries up the orphan's tears?
Is it a king regards the client's cry?
Gives life to him by law condemned to die?
Is it his care the commonwealth that keeps,
As doth the nurse her baby whilst it sleeps?   60
And that poor king of all those hopes prevented,
Unheard, unhelped, unpitied, unlamented?
   Yet let me be with poverty oppressed,
Of earthly blessings robbed and dispossessed,

Let me be scorned, rejected, and reviled,
And from my kingdom let me live exiled,
Let the world's curse upon me still remain,
And let the last bring on the first again;
All miseries that wretched man may wound,
Leave for my comfort only Rosamond.   70
For thee, swift time his speedy course doth stay,
At thy command, the destinies obey;
Pity is dead that comes not from thine eyes,
And at thy feet ev'n mercy prostrate lies.
    If I were feeble, rheumatic, or cold,
These were true signs that I were waxèd old;
But I can march all day in massy steel,
Nor yet my arms' unwieldy weight do feel;
Nor waked by night with bruise or bloody wound,
The tent my bed, no pillow but the ground.   80
For very age had I lain bedrid long,
One smile of thine again could make me young.
Were there in art a power but so divine,
As is in that sweet angel-tongue of thine,
That great enchantress, which once took such pains,
To put young blood into old Aeson's veins,
And in groves, mountains, and the moorish fen,
Sought out more herbs than had been known to men,
And in the powerful potion that she makes,
Put blood of men, of birds, of beasts, and snakes,   90
Never had needed to have gone so far,
To seek the soils where all those simples are;
One accent from thy lips the blood more warms,
Than all her philtres, exorcisms, and charms.
Thy presence hath repairèd in one day,
What many years with sorrows did decay,
And made fresh beauty in her flower to spring,
Out of the wrinkles of time's ruining.
Ev'n as the hungry winter-starvèd earth,
When she by nature labours towards her birth,   100
Still as the day upon the dark world creeps,
One blossom forth after another peeps,

Till the small flower, whose root at last unbound,
Gets from the frosty prison of the ground,
Spreading the leaves unto the powerful noon,
Decked in fresh colours, smiles upon the sun.
　　Never unquiet care lodged in that breast,
Where but one thought of Rosamond did rest;
Nor thirst, nor travail, which on war attend,
E'er brought the long day to desirèd end;　　　　　　　110
Nor yet did pale fear, or lean famine live,
Where hope of thee did any comfort give:
Ah, what injustice then is this of thee,
That thus the guiltless dost condemn for me?
When only she (by means of my offence)
Redeems thy pureness and thy innocence.
When to our wills perforce obey they must,
That's just in them, whate'er in us unjust;
Of what we do, not them, account we make;
The fault craves pardon for th'offender's sake,　　　　120
And what to work a prince's will may merit,
Hath deep'st impression in the gentlest spirit.
　　If't be my name that doth thee so offend,
No more myself shall be mine own name's friend;
If it be that, which thou dost only hate,
That name, in my name, lastly hath his date;
Say 'tis accursed, and fatal, and dispraise it;
If written, blot it, if engraven, raze it;
Say, that of all names 'tis a name of woe,
Once a king's name, but now it is not so:　　　　　　130
And when all this is done, I know 'twill grieve thee;
And therefore, sweet, why should I now believe thee?
　　Nor shouldst thou think those eyes with envy lower,
Which passing by thee, gaze up to thy tower;
But rather praise thine own, which be so clear,
Which from the turret like two stars appear:
Above, the sun doth shine, beneath, thine eye,
Mocking the heav'n, to make another sky.
　　The little stream which by thy tower doth glide,
Where oft thou spend'st the weary evening tide,　　　140

To view thee well, his course would gladly stay,
As loath from thee to part so soon away,
And with salutes thyself would gladly greet,
And offer up some small drops at thy feet;
But finding that the envious banks restrain it,
T'excuse itself, doth in this sort complain it,
And therefore this sad bubbling murmur keeps,
And for thy want within the channel weeps.
And as thou dost into the water look,
The fish which see thy shadow in the brook,   150
Forget to feed, and all amazèd lie,
So daunted with the lustre of thine eye.
    And that sweet name, which thou so much dost wrong,
In time shall be some famous poet's song;
And with the very sweetness of that name,
Lions and tigers men shall learn to tame.
The careful mother, at her pensive breast,
With Rosamond shall bring her babe to rest;
The little birds (by men's continual sound)
Shall learn to speak, and prattle Rosamond: 160
And when in April they begin to sing,
With Rosamond shall welcome in the spring;
And she in whom all rarities are found,
Shall still be said to be a Rosamond.
    The little flowers dropping their honied dew,
Which (as thou writ'st) do weep upon thy shoe,
Not for thy fault, sweet Rosamond, do moan,
Only lament, that thou so soon art gone;
For if thy foot touch hemlock as it goes,
That hemlock's made more sweeter than the rose.   170
    Of Jove, of Neptune, how they did betray,
Speak not; of Io, or Amymone,
When she, for whom Jove once became a bull,
Compared with thee, had been a tawny trull;
He a white bull, and she a whiter cow,
Yet he nor she ne'er half so white as thou.
    Long since, thou know'st, my care provided for
To lodge thee safe from jealous Eleanor,

The labyrinth's conveyance guides thee so,
(Which only Vaughan, thou, and I do know)   180
If she do guard thee with an hundred eyes,
I have an hundred subtle Mercuries,
To watch that Argus which my love doth keep,
Until eye after eye fall all to sleep.

   And those stars which look in, but look to see,
Wond'ring what star here on the earth should be;
As oft the moon, amidst the silent night,
Hath come to joy us with her friendly light,
And by the curtain helped mine eye to see
What envious night and darkness hid from me;   190
When I have wished, that she might ever stay,
And other worlds might still enjoy the day.

   What should I say? Words, tears, and sighs be spent,
And want of time doth further help prevent:
My camp resounds with fearful shocks of war,
Yet in my breast more dang'rous conflicts are;
Yet is my signal to the battle's sound,
The blessèd name of beauteous Rosamond.
Accursèd be that heart, that tongue, that breath,
Should think, should speak, or whisper of thy death;   200
For in one smile, or lower from thy sweet eye,
Consists my life, my hope, my victory.
Sweet Woodstock, where my Rosamond doth rest,
Be blest in her, in whom thy king is blest:
For though in France a while my body be,
My heart remains, dear Paradise, in thee.

THE BARONS' WARS, 1603, 1619

From Canto 6
Within the castle had the queen devised
(Long about which she busied had her thought)
A chamber, wherein she imparadised
What shapes for her could anywhere be sought;
Which in the same were curiously comprised,
By skilful painters excellently wrought:
And in the place of greatest safety there,
Which she had named the Tower of Mortimer.

A room prepared with pilasters she chose,
That to the roof their slender points did rear,   10
Arching the top, whereas they all did close,
Which from below showed like an hemisphere;
In whose concavity she did compose
The constellations that to us appear,
In their corporeal shapes, with stars enchased,
As by th'old poets they on heaven were placed.

About which lodging, tow'rds the upper face,
Ran a fine border, circularly led,
As equal 'twixt the zenith and the base,
Which as a zone the waist engirdlèd,   20
That lent the sight a breathing, by the space
'Twixt things near hand, and those far overhead;
Upon the plain wall of which lower part,
Painting expressed the utmost of her art.

There Phoebus clipping Hyacinthus stood,
Whose life's last drops did the god's breast imbrue,
His tears so mixèd with the young boy's blood,
That whether was the more, no eye could view;
And though together lost as in a flood,
Yet here and there th'one from th'other drew;   30
The pretty wood-nymphs chafing him with balm,
Proving to wake him from his deadly qualm.

Apollo's quiver, and far-killing bow,
His gold-fringed mantle on the grassful ground,
T'express whose act, art ev'n her best did show,
The sledge so shadowed still as to rebound,
As it had scarce done giving of the blow,
Lending a lasting freshness to the wound;
The purple flower from the boy's blood begun,
That since ne'er spreads but to the rising sun.   40

Near that was Io, in a heifer's shape,
Viewing her new-ta'en figure in a brook,
In which, her shadow seemed on her to gape,
As on the same she greedily did look,
To see how Jove could cloud his wanton scape:
So done, that the beholders oft mistook
Themselves; to some, that one way did allow
A woman's likeness, th'other way, a cow.

There Mercury was like a shepherd's boy,
Sporting with Hebe by a fountain brim,   50
With many a sweet glance, many an am'rous toy;
He sprinkling drops at her, and she at him:
Wherein the painter so explained their joy,
As he had meant the very life to limn;
For on their brows he made the drops so clear,
That through each drop their fair skins did appear.

By them, in landskip, rocky Cynthus reared,
With the clouds leaning on his lofty crown,
On his sides showing many a straggling herd,
And from his top, the clear springs creeping down   60
By the old rocks, each with a hoary beard,
With moss and climbing ivy overgrown;
So done, that the beholders with the skill
Never enough their longing eyes could fill.

Th'half-naked nymphs, some climbing, some descending,
The sundry flowers at one another flung,

44

In postures strange, their limber bodies bending;
Some cropping branches that seemed lately sprung,
Upon the brakes their coloured mantles rending,
Which on the mount grew here and there among;   70
Combing their hair some, some made garlands by;
So strove the painter to content the eye.

In one part, Phaethon cast amongst the clouds
By Phoebus' palfreys, that their reins had broke,
His chariot tumbling from the welkèd shrouds,
And the fierce steeds flew madding from their yoke,
The elements confusèdly in crowds,
And heaven and earth were nought but flame and smoke:
A piece so done, that many did desire
To warm themselves, some frighted with the fire.   80

And into Padus falling, as he burned,
Thereinto thrown by Jove, out of the skies;
His weeping sisters, there to trees were turned,
Yet so of women did retain the guise,
That none could censure whether (as they mourned)
Drops from their boughs, or tears fell from their eyes:
Done for the last, with such exceeding life,
As art therein with nature seemed at strife.

And for the light to this brave lodging lent,
The workmen, who as wisely could direct,   90
Did for the same the windows so invent,
That they should artificially reflect
The day alike on ev'ry lineament,
To their proportion and had such respect,
As that the beams, condensated and grave,
To ev'ry figure a sure colour gave.

In part of which, under a golden vine,
Which held a curious canopy through all,
Stood a rich bed quite covered with the twine,
Shadowing the same in the redoubling fall,   100

Whose clusters drew the branches to decline;
'Mongst which did many a naked cupid sprawl:
Some at the sundry-coloured birds did shoot,
And some about to pluck the purple fruit.

On which a tissue counterpoyne was cast
(Arachne's web did not the same surpass)
Wherein the story of his fortunes past
In lively pictures neatly handled was:
How he escaped the Tower, in France how graced,
With stones embroidered, of a wondrous mass;   110
About the border, in a fine-wrought fret,
Emblems, impresas, hieroglyphics set.

This flatt'ring sunshine had begot the shower,
And the black clouds with such abundance fed,
That for a wind they waited but the hour,
With force to let their fury on his head;
Which when it came, it came with such a power,
As he could hardly have imaginèd;
But when men think they most in safety stand,
Their greatest peril often is at hand.   120

For to that largeness they increasèd were,
That Edward felt March heavy on his throne,
Whose props no longer both of them could bear;
Two for one seat that over-great were grown,
Prepost'rously that movèd in one sphere,
And to the like predominancy prone,
That the young king down Mortimer must cast,
If he himself would e'er hope to sit fast.

Who finding the necessity was such
That urged him still th'assault to undertake,   130
And yet his person it might nearly touch,
Should he too soon his sleeping power awake;
Th'attempt wherein the danger was so much
Drove him at length a secret means to make,

Whereby he might the enterprise effect,
And hurt him most, where he did least suspect.

Without the castle, in the earth is found
A cave, resembling sleepy Morpheus' cell,
In strange meanders winding underground,
Where darkness seeks continually to dwell, 140
Which with such fear and horror doth abound,
As though it were an entrance into hell;
By architects to serve the castle made,
When as the Danes this island did invade.

Now on along the crankling path doth keep;
Then by a rock turns up another way;
Rising tow'rds day, then falling tow'rds the deep,
On a smooth level then itself doth lay;
Directly then, then obliquely doth creep,
Nor in the course keeps any certain stay; 150
Till in the castle, in an odd by-place,
It casts the foul mask from its dusky face.

By which, the king with a selected crew,
Of such as he with his intent acquainted,
Which he affected to the action knew,
And in revenge of Edward had not fainted,
That to their utmost would the cause pursue,
And with those treasons that had not been tainted,
Adventurèd the labyrinth t'assay,
To rouse the beast which kept them all at bay. 160

Long after Phoebus took his lab'ring team
To his pale sister and resigned his place,
To wash his couples in the ocean stream,
And cool the fervour of his glowing face;
And Phoebe, scanted of her brother's beam,
Into the west went after him apace,
Leaving black darkness to possess the sky,
To fit the time of that black tragedy.

47

What time, by torch-light they attempt the cave,
Which at their entrance seemed in a fright, 170
With the reflection that their armour gave,
As it till then had ne'er seen any light;
Which striving there pre-eminence to have,
Darkness therewith so daringly doth fight,
That each confounding other, both appear
As darkness light, and light but darkness were.

The craggy cleves, which cross them as they go,
Made as their passage they would have denied,
And threatened them their journey to forslow,
As angry with the path that was their guide, 180
And sadly seemed their discontent to show
To the vile hand that did them first divide;
Whose cumbrous falls and risings seemed to say,
So ill an action could not brook the day.

And by the lights as they along were led,
Their shadows then them following at their back,
Were like to mourners carrying forth their dead,
And as the deed, so were they ugly black,
Or like to fiends that them had followèd,
Pricking them on to bloodshed, and to wrack; 190
Whilst the light looked as it had been amazed,
At their deformèd shapes whereon it gazed.

The clatt'ring arms their masters seemed to chide,
As they would reason wherefore they should wound,
And struck the cave, in passing on each side,
As they were angry with the hollow ground,
That it an act so pitiless should hide;
Whose stony roof locked in their angry sound,
And hanging in the creeks, drew back again,
As willing them from murder to refrain. 200

The night waxed old (not dreaming of these things)
And to her chamber is the queen withdrawn,

To whom a choice musician plays and sings,
Whilst she sat under an estate of lawn,
In night-attire, more god-like glittering,
Than any eye had seen the cheerful dawn,
Leaning upon her most loved Mortimer,
Whose voice, more than the music, pleased her ear.

Where her fair breasts at liberty were let,
Whose violet veins in branchèd riverets flow,   210
And Venus' swans, and milky doves were set
Upon those swelling mounts of driven snow;
Whereon whilst love to sport himself doth get,
He lost his way, nor back again could go,
But with those banks of beauty set about,
He wandered still, yet never could get out.

Her loose hair looked like gold (O word too base!
Nay, more than sin but so to name her hair),
Declining, as to kiss her fairer face;
No word is fair enough for thing so fair,   220
Nor never was there epithet could grace
That, by much praising, which we much impair;
And where the pen fails, pencils cannot show it;
Only the soul may be supposed to know it.

She laid her fingers on his manly cheek,
The gods' pure sceptres, and the darts of love,
That with their touch might make a tiger meek,
Or might great Atlas from his seat remove;
So white, so soft, so delicate, so sleek,
As she had worn a lily for a glove,   230
As might beget life, where was never none,
And put a spirit into the hardest stone.

The fire, of precious wood; the light, perfume,
Which left a sweetness on each thing it shone,
As ev'rything did to itself assume
The scent from them, and made the same their own,

49

So that the painted flowers within the room
Were sweet, as if they naturally had grown;
The light gave colours, which upon them fell,
And to the colours the perfume gave smell.   240

When on those sundry pictures they devise,
And from one piece they to another run,
Commend that face, that arm, that hand, those eyes,
Show how that bird, how well that flower was done;
How this part shadowed, and how that did rise,
This top was clouded, how that trail was spun,
The landskip, mixture, and delineatings,
And in that art, a thousand curious things.

Looking upon proud Phaethon wrapped in fire,
The gentle queen did much bewail his fall;   250
But Mortimer commended his desire,
To lose one poor life, or to govern all:
'What though,' quoth he, 'he madly did aspire,
And his great mind made him proud fortune's thrall?
Yet in despite, when she her worst had done,
He perished in the chariot of the sun.'

Phoebus, she said, was over-forced by art,
Nor could she find how that embrace could be;
But Mortimer then took the painter's part:
'Why thus, bright empress, thus, and thus,' quoth he,   260
'That hand doth hold his back, and this his heart;
Thus their arms twine, and thus their lips, you see;
Now are you Phoebus, Hyacinthus I;
It were a life thus ev'ry hour to die.'

When, by that time, into the castle hall
Was rudely entered that well-armèd rout,
And they within suspecting nought at all,
Had then no guard, to watch for them without:
See how mischances suddenly do fall,
And steal upon us, being farth'st from doubt;   270

50

Our life's uncertain, and our death is sure,
And tow'rds most peril, man is most secure.

Whilst youthful Neville, and brave Turrington,
To the bright queen that ever waited near,
Two, with great March much credit that had won,
That in the lobby with the ladies were,
Staying delight, whilst time away did run,
With such discourse as women love to hear,
Charged on the sudden by the armèd train,
Were at their entrance miserably slain.   280

When, as from snow-crowned Skiddaw's lofty cleves
Some fleet-winged haggard, tow'rds her preying hour,
Amongst the teal and moor-bred mallard drives,
And th'air of all her feathered flocks doth scour,
Whilst to regain her former height she strives,
The fearful fowl all prostrate to her power;
Such a sharp shriek did ring throughout the vault,
Made by the women at the fierce assault.

Unarmed was March (she only in his arms,
Too soft a shield to bear their boist'rous blows)   290
Who least of all suspected such alarms,
And to be so encountered by his foes,
When he was most improvident of harms.
O, had he had but weapons to his woes!
Either his valour had his life redeemed,
Or in her sight died happily esteemed.

ODES, 1606, 1619

To Himself, and the Harp

And why not I, as he
That's greatest, if as free,
(In sundry strains that strive
Since there so many be)
Th'old lyric kind revive?

I will, yea, and I may;
Who shall oppose my way?
For what is he alone
That of himself can say
He's heir of Helicon?   10

Apollo, and the Nine,
Forbid no man their shrine
That cometh with hands pure;
Else they be so divine
They will him not endure.

For they be such coy things
That they care not for kings,
And dare let them know it;
Nor may he touch their springs,
That is not born a poet.   20

The Phocean it did prove,
Whom when foul lust did move
Those maids unchaste to make,
Fell, as with them he strove,
His neck and justly brake.

That instrument ne'er heard,
Struck by the skilful bard,
It strongly to awake,
But it th' infernals scared,
And made Olympus quake.   30

52

As those prophetic strings
Whose sounds with fiery wings
Drave fiends from their abode,
Touched by the best of kings,
That sang the holy ode,

So his, which women slew,
And it into Hebrus threw;
Such sounds yet forth it sent,
The banks to weep that drew,
As down the stream it went.   40

That by the tortoise shell,
To Maya's son it fell;
The most thereof not doubt
But sure some power did dwell,
In him who found it out.

The wildest of the field,
And air, with rivers t'yield
Which moved; that sturdy glebes
And massy oaks could wield
To raise the piles of Thebes.   50

And diversely though strung,
So anciently we sung
To it, that now scarce known
If first it did belong
To Greece, or if our own.

The druidës imbrued
With gore, on altars rude
With sacrifices crowned,
In hollow woods bedewed,
Adored the trembling sound.   60

Though we be all to seek
Of Pindar, that great Greek,

To finger it aright,
The soul with power to strike,
His hand retained such might.

Or him that Rome did grace,
Whose airs we all embrace,
That scarcely found his peer,
Nor giveth Phoebus place
For strokes divinely clear.   70

The Irish I admire,
And still cleave to that lyre,
As our music's mother,
And think, till I expire,
Apollo's such another

As Britons, that so long
Have held this antique song,
And let all our carpers
Forbear their fame to wrong,
That are right skilful harpers.   80

Soowthern, I long thee spare,
Yet wish thee well to fare,
Who me pleased'st greatly,
As first, therefore more rare,
Handling thy harp neatly.

To those that with despite
Shall term these numbers slight,
Tell them their judgment's blind,
Much erring from the right;
It is a noble kind.   90

Nor is't the verse doth make,
That giveth, or doth take;
'Tis possible to climb,
To kindle, or to slake,
Although in Skelton's rhyme.

An Ode Written in the Peak

This while we are abroad
Shall we not touch our lyre?
Shall we not sing an ode?
Shall that holy fire
In us that strongly glowed
In this cold air expire?

Long since the summer laid
Her lusty bravery down;
The autumn half is weighed,
And Boreas 'gins to frown,   10
Since now I did behold
Great Brute's first-builded town.

Though in the utmost Peak
A while we do remain,
Amongst the mountains bleak
Exposed to sleet and rain,
No sport our hours shall break
To exercise our vein.

What though bright Phoebus' beams
Refresh the southern ground,   20
And though the princely Thames
With beauteous nymphs abound,
And by old Camber's streams
Be many wonders found;

Yet many rivers clear
Here glide in silver swathes,
And what of all most dear,
Buxton's delicious baths,
Strong ale and noble cheer,
T'assuage breme winter's scathes.   30

Those grim and horrid caves
Whose looks affright the day,

Wherein nice nature saves
What she would not bewray,
Our better leisure craves,
And doth invite our lay.

In places far or near,
Or famous or obscure,
Where wholesome is the air,
Or where the most impure,   40
All times, and everywhere,
The muse is still in ure.

To the Virginian Voyage

You brave heroic minds
Worthy your country's name,
That honour still pursue,
Go, and subdue,
Whilst loit'ring hinds
Lurk here at home with shame.

Britons, you stay too long;
Quickly aboard bestow you,
And with a merry gale
Swell your stretched sail,   10
With vows as strong
As the winds that blow you.

Your course securely steer,
West and by south forth keep;
Rocks, lee shores, nor shoals,
When Aeolus scowls,
You need not fear,
So absolute the deep.

And cheerfully at sea
Success you still entice   20

To get the pearl and gold,
And ours to hold
Virginia,
Earth's only paradise.

Where nature hath in store
Fowl, venison, and fish,
And the fruitfullest soil,
Without your toil,
Three harvests more,
All greater than your wish. 30

And the ambitious vine
Crowns with his purple mass
The cedar reaching high
To kiss the sky,
The cypress, pine,
And useful sassafras.

To whom the golden age
Still nature's laws doth give;
No other cares attend,
But them to defend 40
From winter's rage,
That long there doth not live.

When as the luscious smell
Of that delicious land
Above the seas that flows
The clear wind throws,
Your hearts to swell
Approaching the dear strand,

In kenning of the shore
(Thanks to God first given) 50
O you the happiest men,
Be frolic then;
Let cannons roar,
Frighting the wide heaven.

And in regions far,
Such heroes bring ye forth
As those from whom we came,
And plant our name
Under that star
Not known unto our North. 60

And as there plenty grows
Of laurel everywhere,
Apollo's sacred tree,
You it may see
A poet's brows
To crown, that may sing there.

Thy *Voyages* attend,
Industrious Hakluyt,
Whose reading shall inflame
Men to see fame, 70
And much commend
To after-times thy wit.

To the Cambro-Britons, and Their Harp, His Ballad of Agincourt

Fair stood the wind for France,
When we our sails advance,
Nor now to prove our chance
Longer will tarry;
But putting to the main,
.At Caux, the mouth of Seine,
With all his martial train,
Landed King Harry.

And taking many a fort,
Furnished in warlike sort, 10
Marcheth tow'rds Agincourt
In happy hour;
Skirmishing day by day

With those that stopped his way
Where the French general lay,
With all his power.

Which in his height of pride,
King Henry to deride,
His ransom to provide
To the king sending;   20
Which he neglects the while,
As from a nation vile,
Yet with an angry smile
Their fall portending.

And turning to his men,
Quoth our brave Henry then,
'Though they to one be ten,
Be not amazèd.
Yet have we well begun;
Battles so bravely won   30
Have ever to the sun
By fame been raisèd.

'And for myself,' quoth he,
'This my full rest shall be;
England ne'er mourn for me,
Nor more esteem me.
Victor I will remain,
Or on this earth lie slain;
Never shall she sustain
Loss to redeem me.   40

'Poitiers and Crécy tell
When most their pride did swell,
Under our swords they fell;
No less our skill is,
Than when our grandsire great,
Claiming the regal seat,
By many a warlike feat
Lopped the French lilies.'

The Duke of York so dread
The eager vaward led;
With the main Henry sped
Amongst his henchmen.
Exeter had the rear,
A braver man not there;
O Lord, how hot they were
On the false Frenchmen!

They now to fight are gone,
Armour on armour shone,
Drum now to drum did groan,
To hear was wonder;
That with the cries they make
The very earth did shake;
Trumpet to trumpet spake,
Thunder to thunder.

Well it thine age became,
O noble Erpingham,
Which didst the signal aim
To our hid forces;
When from a meadow by,
Like a storm suddenly, 70
The English archery
Stuck the French horses.

With Spanish yew so strong,
Arrows a cloth-yard long
That like to serpents stung,
Piercing the weather,
None from his fellow starts,
But playing manly parts,
And like true English hearts,
Stuck close together. 80

When down their bows they threw,
And forth their bilboes drew,

And on the French they flew,
Not one was tardy;
Arms were from shoulders sent,
Scalps to the teeth were rent,
Down the French peasants went;
Our men were hardy.

This while our noble king,
His broad sword brandishing, 90
Down the French host did ding,
As to o'erwhelm it;
And many a deep wound lent,
His arms with blood besprent,
And many a cruel dent
Bruisèd his helmet.

Gloucester, that duke so good,
Next of the royal blood,
For famous England stood,
With his brave brother; 100
Clarence, in steel so bright,
Though but a maiden knight,
Yet in that furious fight
Scarce such another.

Warwick in blood did wade,
Oxford the foe invade,
And cruel slaughter made
Still as they ran up;
Suffolk his axe did ply,
Beaumont and Willoughby 110
Bare them right doughtily,
Ferrers and Fanhope.

Upon Saint Crispin's day
Fought was this noble fray,
Which fame did not delay
To England to carry;

O, when shall English men
With such acts fill a pen,
Or England breed again
Such a King Harry?   120

To His Rival

Her loved I most,
By thee that's lost,
Though she were won with leisure;
She was my gain,
But to my pain,
Thou spoil'st me of my treasure.

The ship full fraught
With gold far sought,
Though ne'er so wisely helmèd,
May suffer wrack   10
In sailing back,
By tempest overwhelmèd.

But she, good sir,
Did not prefer
You, for that I was ranging;
But for that she
Found faith in me,
And she loved to be changing.

Therefore boast not
Your happy lot,   20
Be silent now you have her;
The time I knew
She slighted you,
When I was in her favour.

None stands so fast
But may be cast

By fortune, and disgracèd;
Once did I wear
Her garter there,
Where you her glove have placèd.   30

I had the vow
That thou hast now,
And glances to discover
Her love to me,
And she to thee
Reads but old lessons over.

She hath no smile
That can beguile,
But as my thought I know it;
Yea, to a hair,   40
Both when and where
And how she will bestow it.

What now is thine
Was only mine,
And first to me was given;
Thou laugh'st at me,
I laugh at thee,
And thus we two are even.

But I'll not mourn,
But stay my turn;   50
The wind may come about, sir,
And once again
May bring me in,
And help to bear you out, sir.

FROM *POLY-OLBION*, 1612, 1622

From Song 6
    When as the salmon seeks a fresher stream to find
(Which hither from the sea comes yearly by his kind,
As he in season grows) and stems the wat'ry tract
Where Teifi falling down doth make a cataract,
Forced by the rising rocks that there her course oppose,
As though within their bounds they meant her to enclose;
Here, when the labouring fish doth at the foot arrive,
And finds that by his strength but vainly he doth strive,
His tail takes in his teeth; and bending like a bow
That's to the compass drawn, aloft himself doth throw: 10
Then springing at his height, as doth a little wand
That bended end to end, and flirted from the hand,
Far off itself doth cast; so doth the salmon vault.
And if at first he fail, his second somersault
He instantly assays; and from his nimble ring,
Still yerking, never leaves, until himself he fling
Above the streamful top of the surrounded heap.
    More famous long agone than for the salmon's leap,
For beavers Teifi was, in her strong banks that bred,
Which else no other brook of Britain nourishèd: 20
Where nature in the shape of this now-perished beast
His property did seem t'have wondrously expressed;
Being bodied like a boat, with such a mighty tail
As served him for a bridge, a helm, or for a sail,
When kind did him command the architect to play,
That his strong castle built of branchèd twigs and clay:
Which, set upon the deep, but yet not fixèd there,
He easily could remove as it he pleased to steer
To this side or to that; the workmanship so rare.
His stuff wherewith to build first being to prepare,   30
A-foraging he goes, to groves or bushes nigh,
And with his teeth cuts down his timber: which laid by,
He turns him on his back, his belly laid abroad,
When with what he hath got, the other do him load,
Till lastly by the weight, his burthen he have found.

Then, with his mighty tail his carriage having bound
As carters do with ropes, in his sharp teeth he gripped
Some stronger stick: from which the lesser branches stripped,
He takes it in the midst; at both the ends, the rest
Hard holding with their fangs, unto the labour pressed,   40
Going backward, tow'rds their home their loaded carriage led;
From whom, those first here born were taught the useful sled.
Then builded he his fort with strong and several fights;
His passages contrived with such unusual sleights,
That from the hunter oft he issued undiscerned,
As if men from this beast to fortify had learned.

From Song 7
When soon the goodly Wyre, that wonted was so high
Her stately top to rear, ashamèd to behold
Her straight and goodly woods unto the furnace sold
(And looking on herself, by her decay doth see
The misery wherein her sister forests be)
Of Erysicthon's end begins her to bethink,
And of his cruel plagues doth wish they all might drink
That thus have them despoiled: then of her own despite,
That she, in whom her town, fair Bewdley, took delight,
And from her goodly seat conceived so great a pride,   10
In Severn on her east, Wyre on the setting side,
So naked left of woods, of pleasure, and forlorn,
As she that loved her most, her now the most doth scorn;
With endless grief perplexed, her stubborn breast she strake,
And to the deafened air thus passionately spake:
    'You dryads, that are said with oaks to live and die,
Wherefore in our distress do you our dwellings fly,
Upon this monstrous age and not revenge our wrong?
For cutting down an oak that justly did belong
To one of Ceres' nymphs, in Thessaly that grew   20
In the Dodonean grove, O nymphs, you could pursue
The son of Perops then, and did the goddess stir
That villainy to wreak the tyrant did to her:
Who, with a dreadful frown did blast the growing grain,
And having from him reft what should his life maintain,

She unto Scythia sent for Hunger, him to gnaw,
And thrust her down his throat, into his staunchless maw;
Who, when nor sea nor land for him sufficient were,
With his devouring teeth his wretched flesh did tear.

    This did you for one tree; but of whole forests they   30
That in these impious times have been the vile decay
(Whom I may justly call their country's deadly foes)
'Gainst them you move no power, their spoil unpunished goes.
How many grievèd souls in future time shall starve
For that which they have raped, their beastly lust to serve!

    We, sometime that the state of famous Britain were,
For whom she was renowned in kingdoms far and near,
Are ransacked; and our trees so hacked above the ground,
That where their lofty tops their neighbouring countries crowned,
Their trunks (like agèd folks) now bare and naked stand,   40
As for revenge to heaven each held a withered hand;
And where the goodly herds of high-palmed harts did gaze
Upon the passer-by, there now doth only graze
The galled-back carrion jade, and hurtful swine do spoil
Once to the sylvan powers our consecrated soil.

From Song 13
When Phoebus lifts his head out of the winter's wave,
No sooner doth the earth her flowery bosom brave,
At such time as the year brings on the pleasant spring,
But hunts-up to the morn the feathered sylvans sing;
And in the lower grove, as on the rising knoll,
Upon the highest spray of every mounting pole,
Those quiristers are perched with many a speckled breast.
Then from her burnished gate the goodly glitt'ring east
Gilds every lofty top, which late the humorous night
Bespangled had with pearl, to please the morning's sight: 10
On which the mirthful choirs, with their clear open throats,
Unto the joyful morn so strain their warbling notes,
That hills and valleys ring, and even the echoing air
Seems all composed of sounds, about them everywhere.
The throstle, with shrill sharps, as purposely he song
T'awake the lustless sun; or chiding, that so long

He was in coming forth, that should the thickets thrill:
The ouzel near at hand, that hath a golden bill,
As nature him had marked of purpose, t'let us see
That from all other birds his tunes should different be: 20
For, with their vocal sounds, they sing to pleasant May;
Upon his dulcet pipe the merle doth only play.
When in the lower brake, the nightingale hard by,
In such lamenting strains the joyful hours doth ply,
As though the other birds she to her tunes would draw.
And, but that nature (by her all-constraining law)
Each bird to her own kind this season doth invite,
They else alone to hear that charmer of the night
(The more to use their ears) their voices sure would spare,
That moduleth her tunes so admirably rare,   30
As man to set in parts, at first had learned of her.
    To Philomel the next, the linnet we prefer;
And by that warbling bird, the wood-lark place we then,
The reed-sparrow, the nope, the red-breast, and the wren,
The yellow-pate; which though she hurt the blooming tree,
Yet scarce hath any bird a finer pipe than she.
And of these chanting fowls, the goldfinch not behind,
That hath so many sorts descending from her kind.
The tydie for her notes as delicate as they,
The laughing hecco, then the counterfeiting jay,   40
The softer with the shrill (some hid among the leaves,
Some in the taller trees, some in the lower greaves)
Thus sing away the morn, until the mounting sun
Through thick exhalèd fogs his golden head hath run,
And through the twisted tops of our close covert creeps
To kiss the gentle shade, this while that sweetly sleeps.

From Song 23
The man whose vacant mind prepares him to the sport,
The finder sendeth out, to seek out nimble Wat,
Which crosseth in the field, each furlong, every flat,
Till he this pretty beast upon the form hath found;
Then viewing for the course, which is the fairest ground,
The greyhounds forth are brought, for coursing then in case,

And choicely in the slip, one leading forth a brace,
The finder puts her up, and gives her coursers law.
And whilst the eager dogs upon the start do draw,
She riseth from her seat, as though on earth she flew,   10
Forced by some yelping cut to give the greyhounds view,
Which are at length let slip, when gunning out they go,
As in respect of them the swiftest wind were slow;
When each man runs his horse, with fixèd eyes, and notes
Which dog first turns the hare, which first the other cotes.
They wrench her once or twice, ere she a turn will take;
What's offered by the first, the other good doth make;
And turn for turn again with equal speed they ply,
Bestirring their swift feet with strange agility.
A hardened ridge or way, when if the hare do win,   20
Then as shot from a bow, she from the dogs doth spin,
That strive to put her off, but when he cannot reach her,
This giving him a cote, about again doth fetch her
To him that comes behind, which seems the hare to bear;
But with a nimble turn she casts them both arrear;
Till oft for want of breath to fall to ground they make her,
The greyhounds both so spent, that they want breath to take her.

From Song 26
In this our spacious isle, I think there is not one
But he hath heard some talk of him and Little John;
And to the end of time, the tales shall ne'er be done
Of Scarlock, George-a-Greene, and Much the Miller's son,
Of Tuck the merry friar, which many a sermon made
In praise of Robin Hood, his outlaws, and their trade.
An hundred valiant men had this brave Robin Hood,
Still ready at his call, that bowmen were right good,
All clad in Lincoln green, with caps of red and blue;
His fellows winded horn, not one of them but knew,   10
When setting to their lips their little bugles shrill,
The warbling echoes waked from every dale and hill.
Their baldrics set with studs, athwart their shoulders cast,
To which, under their arms their sheaves were buckled fast,
A short sword at their belt, a buckler scarce a span,

Who struck below the knee, not counted then a man.
All made of Spanish yew, their bows were wondrous strong;
They not an arrow drew, but was a cloth-yard long.
Of archery they had the very perfect craft,
With broad-arrow, or butt, or prick, or roving shaft;   20
At marks full forty score they used to prick and rove,
Yet higher than the breast for compass never strove;
Yet at the farthest mark a foot could hardly win;
At long-butts, short, and hoyles, each one could cleave the pin.
Their arrows finely paired, for timber and for feather,
With birch and brazil pieced, to fly in any weather;
And shot they with the round, the square, or forkèd pile,
The loose gave such a twang, as might be heard a mile.
And of these archers brave, there was not any one
But he could kill a deer his swiftest speed upon,   30
Which they did boil and roast, in many a mighty wood,
Sharp hunger the fine sauce to their more kingly food.
Then taking them to rest, his merry men and he
Slept many a summer's night under the greenwood tree.
From wealthy abbots' chests, and churls' abundant store,
What oftentimes he took, he shared amongst the poor:
No lordly bishop came in lusty Robin's way,
To him before he went, but for his pass must pay.
The widow in distress he graciously relieved,
And remedied the wrongs of many a virgin grieved.   40
He from the husband's bed no married woman wan,
But to his mistress dear, his lovèd Marian
Was ever constant known, which wheresoe'er she came,
Was sovereign of the woods, chief lady of the game:
Her clothes tucked to the knee, and dainty braided hair,
With bow and quiver armed, she wandered here and there
Amongst the forests wild; Diana never knew
Such pleasures, nor such harts as Mariana slew.

To My Most Dearly Loved Friend Henry Reynolds, Esquire,
of Poets and Poesy

My dearly lovèd friend, how oft have we
In winter evenings (meaning to be free)
To some well-chosen place used to retire,
And there with moderate meat, and wine, and fire,
Have passed the hours contentedly with chat;
Now talked of this, and then discoursed of that,
Spoke our own verses 'twixt ourselves, if not
Other men's lines, which we by chance had got,
Or some stage pieces famous long before,
Of which your happy memory had store;   10
And I remember you much pleasèd were,
Of those who livèd long ago to hear,
As well as of those of these latter times
Who have enriched our language with their rhymes,
And in succession, how still up they grew,
Which is the subject that I now pursue.
For from my cradle you must know that I
Was still inclined to noble poesy,
And when that once *Pueriles* I had read,
And newly had my Cato construèd,   20
In my small self I greatly marvelled then,
Amongst all other, what strange kind of men
These poets were; and pleasèd with the name,
To my mild tutor merrily I came
(For I was then a proper goodly page,
Much like a pigmy, scarce ten years of age),
Clasping my slender arms about his thigh.
'O my dear master, cannot you,' quoth I,
'Make me a poet? Do it, if you can,
And you shall see, I'll quickly be a man.'   30
Who me thus answered smiling, 'Boy,' quoth he,
'If you'll not play the wag, but I may see
You ply your learning, I will shortly read

70

Some poets to you.' Phoebus be my speed,
Too't hard went I, when shortly he began,
And first read to me honest Mantuan,
Then Virgil's *Eclogues*; being entered thus,
Methought I straight had mounted Pegasus,
And in his full career could make him stop,
And bound upon Parnassus bi-cleft top.   40
I scorned your ballad then, though it were done
And had for *finis*, William Elderton.
But soft, in sporting with this childish jest,
I from my subject have too long digressed;
Then to the matter that we took in hand:
Jove and Apollo for the Muses stand.
    That noble Chaucer, in those former times,
The first enriched our English with his rhymes,
And was the first of ours that ever brake
Into the Muses' treasure, and first spake   50
In weighty numbers, delving in the mine
Of perfect knowledge, which he could refine,
And coin for current, and as much as then
The English language could express to men,
He made it do; and by his wondrous skill,
Gave us much light from his abundant quill.
    And honest Gower, who in respect of him
Had only sipped at Aganippe's brim,
And though in years this last was him before,
Yet fell he far short of the other's store.   60
    When after those, four ages very near,
They with the Muses which conversèd were
That princely Surrey, early in the time
Of the eighth Henry, who was then the prime
Of England's noble youth; with him there came
Wyatt, with reverence whom we still do name
Amongst our poets; Bryan had a share
With the two former, which accounted are
The time's best makers, and the authors were
Of those small poems, which the title bear   70
Of songs and sonnets, wherein oft they hit

On many dainty passages of wit.
  Gascoigne and Churchyard after them again,
In the beginning of Eliza's reign,
Accounted were great meterers many a day,
But not inspired with brave fire; had they
Lived but a little longer, they had seen
Their works before them to have buried been.
    Grave moral Spenser after these came on,
Than whom I am persuaded there was none,   80
Since the blind bard his Iliads up did make,
Fitter a task like that to undertake,
To set down boldly, bravely to invent,
In all high knowledge surely excellent.
    The noble Sidney with this last arose,
That hero for numbers, and for prose,
That throughly paced our language as to show
The plenteous English hand in hand might go
With Greek and Latin, and did first reduce
Our tongue from Lyly's writing then in use,   90
Talking of stones, stars, plants, of fishes, flies,
Playing with words, and idle similes.
As th'English apes and very zanies be
Of everything that they do hear and see,
So imitating his ridiculous tricks,
They spake and writ all like mere lunatics.
    Then Warner, though his lines were not so trimmed,
Nor yet his poem so exactly limned
And neatly jointed, but the critic may
Easily reprove him, yet thus let me say   100
For my old friend, some passages there be
In him, which I protest have taken me
With almost wonder; so fine, clear, and new,
As yet they have been equallèd by few.
    Neat Marlowe, bathèd in the Thespian springs,
Had in him those brave translunary things
That the first poets had; his raptures were
All air, and fire, which made his verses clear;
For that fine madness still he did retain,

Which rightly should possess a poet's brain. 110
    And surely Nashe, though he a proser were,
A branch of laurel yet deserves to bear;
Sharply satiric was he, and that way
He went, since that his being, to this day
Few have attempted, and I surely think
Those words shall hardly be set down with ink
Shall scorch and blast, so as his could, where he
Would inflict vengeance; and be it said of thee,
Shakespeare, thou hadst as smooth a comic vein,
Fitting the sock, and in thy natural brain, 120
As strong conception, and as clear a rage,
As anyone that trafficked with the stage.
    Amongst these Samuel Daniel, whom if I
May spake of, but to censure do deny,
Only have heard some wise men him rehearse
To be too much historian in verse;
His rhymes were smooth, his metres well did close,
But yet his manner better fitted prose.
Next these, learn'd Jonson in this list I bring,
Who had drunk deep of the Pierian spring, 130
Whose knowledge did him worthily prefer,
And long was lord here of the theatre;
Who in opinion made our learn'st to stick,
Whether in poems rightly dramatic,
Strong Seneca or Plautus, he or they,
Should bear the buskin or the sock away.
Others again here livèd in my days,
That have of us deservèd no less praise
For their translations than the daintiest wit
That on Parnassus thinks he high'st doth sit, 140
And for a chair may 'mongst the Muses call,
As the most curious maker of them all:
As reverent Chapman, who hath brought to us,
Musaeus, Homer, and Hesiodus
Out of the Greek, and by his skill hath reared
Them to that height, and to our tongue endeared,
That were those poets at this day alive,

To see their books thus with us to survive,
They would think, having neglected them so long,
They had been written in the English tongue.   150
    And Sylvester, who from the French more weak,
Made Bartas of his six days' labour speak
In natural English; who, had he there stayed,
He had done well, and never had bewrayed
His own invention to have been so poor,
Who still wrote less, in striving to write more.
    Then dainty Sandys, that hath to English done
Smooth-sliding Ovid, and hath made him run
With so much sweetness and unusual grace,
As though the neatness of the English pace   160
Should tell the jetting Latin that it came
But slowly after, as though stiff and lame.
    So Scotland sent us hither, for our own,
That man whose name I ever would have known
To stand by mine, that most ingenious knight,
My Alexander, to whom in his right
I want extremely, yet in speaking thus,
I do but show the love that was 'twixt us,
And not his numbers, which were brave and high,
So like his mind was his clear poesy;   170
And my dear Drummond, to whom much I owe
For his much love, and proud I was to know
His poesy; for which two worthy men,
I Menstrie still shall love, and Hawthornden.
Then the two Beaumonts and my Browne arose,
My dear companions, whom I freely chose
My bosom friends, and in their several ways
Rightly born poets, and in these last days
Men of much note, and no less nobler parts,
Such as have freely told to me their hearts,   180
As I have mine to them. But if you shall
Say in your knowledge that these be not all
Have writ in numbers, be informed that I
Only myself to these few men do tie,
Whose works oft printed, set on every post,

To public censure subject have been most;
For such whose poems, be they ne'er so rare,
In private chambers that encloistered are,
And by transcription daintily must go,
As though the world unworthy were to know   190
Their rich composures, let those men that keep
These wondrous reliques in their judgment deep,
And cry them up so, let such pieces be
Spoke of by those that shall come after me.
I pass not for them, nor do mean to run
In quest of these, that them applause have won
Upon our stages in these latter days,
That are so many; let them have their bays
That do deserve it; let those wits that haunt
Those public circuits, let them freely chant   200
Their fine composures, and their praise pursue;
And so, my dear friend, for this time adieu.

NYMPHIDIA, THE COURT OF FAERY, 1627

Lines 129-280

Her chariot ready straight is made,
Each thing therein is fitting laid,
That she by nothing might be stayed,
For naught must her be letting;
Four nimble gnats the horses were,
Their harnesses of gossamer,
Fly Cranion her charioteer,
Upon the coach-box getting.

Her chariot of a snail's fine shell,
Which for the colours did excel,   10
The fair Queen Mab becoming well,
So lively was the limning;
The seat the soft wool of the bee,
The cover (gallantly to see)

The wing of a pied butterflee;
I trow 'twas simple trimming.

The wheels composed of crickets' bones,
And daintily made for the nonce,
For fear of rattling on the stones,
With thistle-down they shod it;   20
For all her maidens much did fear,
If Oberon had chanced to hear
That Mab his queen should have been there,
He would not have abode it.

She mounts her chariot with a trice,
Nor would she stay for no advice,
Until her maids that were so nice,
To wait on her were fitted,
But ran herself away alone;
Which when they heard, there was not one   30
But hasted after to be gone,
As she had been diswitted.

Hop and Mop and Drop so clear,
Pip and Trip and Skip that were
To Mab their sovereign ever dear,
Her special maids of honour;
Fib and Tib and Pink and Pin,
Tick and Quick and Jill and Jin,
Tit and Nit and Wap and Win,
The train that wait upon her.   40

Upon a grasshopper they got,
And what with amble and with trot,
For hedge nor ditch they sparèd not,
But after her they hie them.
A cobweb over them they throw,
To shield the wind if it should blow;
Themselves they wisely could bestow,
Lest any should espy them.

But let us leave Queen Mab a while,
Through many a gate, o'er many a stile,
That now had gotten by this while,
Her dear Pigwiggen kissing.
And tell how Oberon doth fare,
Who grew as mad as any hare,
When he had sought each place with care,
And found his queen was missing.

                                                  50

By grisly Pluto he doth swear;
He rent his clothes and tore his hair,
And as he runneth, here and there,
An acorn cup he greeteth;
Which soon he taketh by the stalk,
About his head he lets it walk,
Nor doth he any creature balk,
But lays on all he meeteth.

                                                  60

The Tuscan poet doth advance
The frantic paladin of France,
And those more ancient do enhance
Alcides in his fury,
And others Ajax Telamon,
But to this time there hath been none
So bedlam as our Oberon,
Of which I dare assure you.

                                                  70

NOAH'S FLOOD, 1630

Lines 265-360
And now the beasts are walking from the wood,
As well of ravin, as that chew the cud,
The king of beasts his fury doth suppress,
And to the ark leads down the lioness;
The bull for his belovèd mate doth low,
And to the ark brings on the fair-eyed cow;
The stately courser for his mare doth neigh,

And tow'rds the new ark guideth her the way;
The wreathed-horned ram his safety doth pursue,
And to the ark ushers his gentle ewe;   10
The bristly boar, who with his snout up ploughed
The spacious plains, and with his grunting loud
Raised rattling echoes all the woods about,
Leaves his dark den, and having scented out
Noah's new-built ark, in with his sow doth come,
And sty themselves up in a little room.
The hart with his dear hind, the buck and doe,
Leaving their wildness, bring the tripping roe
Along with them; and from the mountain steep
The clamb'ring goat and cony, used to keep   20
Amongst the cleves, together get, and they
To this great ark find out the ready way.
Th'unwieldy elk, whose skin is of much proof,
Throngs with the rest t'attain this wooden roof;
The unicorn leaves off his pride, and close
There sets him down by the rhinoceros;
The elephant there coming to embark,
And as he softly getteth up the ark,
Feeling by his great weight, his body sunk,
Holds by his huge tooth and his nervy trunk;   30
The crook-backed camel climbing to the deck
Draws up himself with his long sinewy neck.
The spotted panther, whose delicious scent
Oft causeth beasts his harbour to frequent,
But having got them once into his power,
Sucketh their blood, and doth their flesh devour,
His cruelty hath quickly cast aside,
And waxing courteous, doth become their guide,
And brings into this universal shop
The ounce, the tiger, and the antelope.   40
By the grim wolf, the poor sheep safely lay,
And was his care, which lately was his prey;
The ass upon the lion leant his head,
And to the cat the mouse for succour fled;
The silly hare doth cast aside her fear,

And forms herself fast by the ugly bear,
At whom the watchful dog did never bark,
When he espied him clamb'ring up the ark.
The fox got in, his subtleties hath left,
And as ashamèd of his former theft,
Sadly sits there, as though he did repent,
And in the ark became an innocent.
The fine-furred ermine, marten, and the cat
That voideth civet, there together sat
By the shrewd monkey, babian, and the ape,
With the hyena, much their like in shape,
Which by their kind are ever doing ill,
Yet in the ark sit civilly and still.
The skipping squirrel of the forest free,
That leapt so nimbly betwixt tree and tree,
Itself into the ark then nimbly cast,
As 'twere a ship-boy come to climb the mast.
The porcupine into the ark doth make,
Nor his sharp quills, though angry, once doth shake;
The sharp-fanged beaver, whose wide-gaping jaw
Cutteth down plants as it were with a saw,
Whose body poisèd, weigheth such a mass,
As though his bowels were of lead or brass,
His cruel chaps, though breathless, he doth close,
As with the rest into the ark he goes.
Th'uneven-legged badger (whose eye-pleasing skin
The case to many a curious thing hath bin
Since that great flood) his fortresses forsakes
Wrought in the earth, and though but halting, makes
Up to the ark; the otter then that keeps
In the wild rivers, in their banks and sleeps,
And feeds on fish, which under water still
He with his kelled feet and keen teeth doth kill,
The other two into the ark doth follow,
Though his ill shape doth cause him but to wallow.
The tortoise and the hedgehog both so slow,
As in their motion scarce discerned to go,
Good footmen grown, contrary to their kind,

50

60

70

80

Lest from the rest they should be left behind;
The rooting mole as to foretell the flood,
Comes out of th'earth, and clambers up the wood;
The little dormouse leaves her leaden sleep,
And with the mole up to the ark doth creep,
With many other, which were common then,
Their kind decayed, but now unknown to men,   90
For there was none, that Adam ere did name,
But to the ark from every quarter came;
By two and two the male and female beast,
From th' swift'st to th' slowest, from greatest to the least,
And as within the strong pale of a park,
So were they all together in the ark.

THE MUSES' ELIZIUM, 1630

From the second nymphal

Lalus.   With full-leaved lilies I will stick
        Thy braided hair all o'er so thick,
        That from it a light shall throw
        Like the sun's upon the snow.
        Thy mantle shall be violet leaves,
        With the fin'st the silkworm weaves
        As finely woven; whose rich smell
        The air about thee so shall swell
        That it shall have no power to move.
        A ruff of pinks thy robe above   10
        About thy neck so neatly set
        That art it cannot counterfet,
        Which still shall look so fresh and new,
        As if upon their roots they grew;
        And for thy head I'll have a tire
        Of netting, made of strawberry wire,
        And in each knot that doth compose
        A mesh, shall stick a half-blown rose,
        Red, damask, white, in order set;
        About the sides shall run a fret   20

Of primroses, the tire throughout
With thrift and daisies fringed about.
All this, fair nymph, I'll do for thee,
So thou'lt leave him and go with me.

Cleon. These be but weeds and trash he brings,
I'll give thee solid, costly things;
His will wither and be gone
Before thou well canst put them on;
With coral I will have thee crowned,
Whose branches intricately wound   30
Shall girt thy temples every way;
And on the top of every spray
Shall stick a pearl orient and great,
Which so the wand'ring birds shall cheat,
That some shall stoop to look for cherries,
As other for tralucent berries,
And wond'ring, caught ere they be ware
In the curled trammels of thy hair.
And for thy neck a crystal chain
Whose links shaped like to drops of rain,   40
Upon thy panting breast depending,
Shall seem as they were still descending,
And as thy breath doth come and go,
So seeming still to ebb and flow;
With amber bracelets cut like bees,
Whose strange transparency who sees,
With silk small as the spider's twist
Doubled so oft about thy wrist,
Would surely think alive they were,
From lilies gathering honey there.   50
Thy buskins ivory, carved like shells
Of scallop, which as little bells
Made hollow, with the air shall chime,
And to thy steps shall keep the time.
Leave Lalus, Lirope, for me
And these shall thy rich dowry be.

Lirope.   Lalus for flowers, Cleon for gems,
           For garlands and for diadems,
           I shall be sped: why, this is brave;
           What nymph can choicer presents have?   60
           With dressing, braiding, frouncing, flow'ring,
           All your jewels on me pouring,
           In this bravery being dressed,
           To the ground I shall be pressed,
           That I doubt the nymphs will fear me,
           Nor will venture to come near me;
           Never Lady of the May,
           To this hour was half so gay;
           All in flowers, all so sweet,
           From the crown, beneath the feet,   70
           Amber, coral, ivory, pearl.
           If this cannot win a girl,
           There's nothing can, and this ye woo me.
           Give me your hands and trust ye to me,
           (Yet to tell ye I am loath)
           That I'll have neither of you both.

Lalus.   When thou shalt please to stem the flood,
           (As thou art of the wat'ry brood)
           I'll have twelve swans more white than snow,
           Yoked for the purpose two and two,   80
           To draw thy barge wrought of fine reed
           So well that it nought else shall need.
           The traces by which they shall hale
           Thy barge shall be the winding trail
           Of woodbind; whose brave tasseled flowers
           (The sweetness of the wood-nymphs' bowers)
           Shall be the trappings to adorn
           The swans, by which thy barge is borne.
           Of flowered flags I'll rob the bank
           Of water-cans and kingcups rank   90
           To be the covering of thy boat,
           And on the stream as thou dost float,
           The naiadës that haunt the deep,

Themselves about thy barge shall keep,
Recording most delightful lays,
By sea gods written in thy praise.
And in what place thou hap'st to land,
There the gentle silvery sand
Shall soften, curlèd with the air
As sensible of thy repair.   100
This, my dear love, I'll do for thee,
So thou'lt leave him and go with me.

Cleon.   Tush, nymph, his swans will prove but geese,
His barge drink water like a fleece;
A boat is base, I'll thee provide
A chariot, wherein Jove may ride;
In which when bravely thou art borne,
Thou shalt look like the glorious morn
Ushering the sun, and such a one
As to this day was never none,   110
Of the rarest Indian gums,
More precious than your balsamums,
Which I by art have made so hard,
That they with tools may well be carved
To make a coach of; which shall be
Materials of this one for thee.
And of thy chariot each small piece
Shall inlaid be with ambergris,
And gilded with the yellow ore
Produced from Tagus' wealthy shore;   120
In which along the pleasant lawn,
With twelve white stags thou shalt be drawn,
Whose branched palms of a stately height,
With several nosegays shall be dight;
And as thou rid'st, thy coach about,
For thy strong guard shall run a rout
Of estridges, whose curlèd plumes,
Censed with thy chariot's rich perfumes,
The scent into the air shall throw;
Whose naked thighs shall grace the show;   130

Whilst the wood-nymphs and those bred
Upon the mountains, o'er thy head
Shall bear a canopy of flowers,
Tinselled with drops of April showers,
Which shall make more glorious shows
Than spangles, or your silver oes.
This, bright nymph, I'll do for thee,
So thou'lt leave him and go with me.

Lirope. Vie and revie, like chapmen proffered,
Would't be received what you have offered; 140
Ye greater honour cannot do me,
If not building altars to me:
Both by water and by land,
Barge and chariot at command,
Swans upon the stream to taw me,
Stags upon the land to draw me.
In all this pomp should I be seen,
What a poor thing were a queen!
All delights in such excess,
As but ye, who can express?
Thus mounted should the nymphs me see,
All the troop would follow me,
Thinking by this state that I
Would assume a deity.
There be some in love have bin,
And I may commit that sin,
And if e'er I be in love,
With one of you I fear 'twill prove,
But with which I cannot tell;
So, my gallant youths, farewell.

From the tenth nymphal
Satyr. O, never ask how I came to this place;
What cannot strong necessity find out?
Rather bemoan my miserable case,
Constrained to wander this wide world about.
With wild Silvanus and his woody crew,

In forests I, at liberty and free,
Lived in such pleasure as the world ne'er knew,
Nor any rightly can conceive but we.
This jocund life we many a day enjoyed,
Till this last age those beastly men forth brought   10
That all those great and goodly woods destroyed,
Whose growth their grandsires with such sufferance sought.
That fair Felicia which was but of late
Earth's paradise, that never had her peer,
Stands now in that most lamentable state,
That not a sylvan will inhabit there,
Where in the soft and most delicious shade
In heat of summer we were wont to play,
When the long day too short for us we made,
The sliding hours so slyly stole away.   20
By Cynthia's light, and on the pleasant lawn,
The wanton faery we were wont to chase,
Which to the nimble cloven-footed fawn
Upon the plain durst boldly bid the base.
The sportive nymphs with shouts and laughter shook
The hills and valleys in their wanton play,
Waking the echoes, their last words that took,
Till at the last they louder were than they.
The lofty high wood, and the lower spring,
Shelt'ring the deer in many a sudden shower,   30
Where choirs of birds oft wonted were to sing,
The flaming furnace wholly doth devour.
Once fair Felicia, but now quite defaced,
Those braveries gone wherein she did abound,
With dainty groves when she was highly graced
With goodly oak, ash, elm, and beeches crowned.
But that from heaven their judgment blinded is,
In human reason it could never be
But that they might have clearly seen by this
Those plagues their next posterity shall see.   40
The little infant on the mother's lap
For want of fire shall be so sore distressed,
That whilst it draws the lank and empty pap,

85

The tender lips shall freeze unto the breast;
The quaking cattle which their warm stall want,
And with bleak winter's northern wind oppressed,
Their browse and stover waxing thin and scant,
The hungry crows shall with their carrion feast.
Men wanting timber wherewith they should build,
And not a forest in Felicia found,   50
Shall be enforced upon the open field
To dig them caves for houses in the ground;
The land thus robbed of all her rich attire,
Naked and bare herself to heaven doth show,
Begging from thence that Jove would dart his fire
Upon those wretches that disrobed her so.
This beastly brood by no means may abide
The name of their brave ancestors to hear,
By whom their sordid slavery is descried,
So unlike them as though not theirs they were;   60
Nor yet they sense nor understanding have
Of those brave muses that their country song,
But with false lips ignobly do deprave
The right and honour that to them belong.
This cruel kind thus viper-like devour
The fruitful soil which them too fully fed;
The earth doth curse the age, and every hour
Again, that it these vip'rous monsters bred.
I, seeing the plagues that shortly are to come
Upon this people, clearly them forsook,   70
And thus am light into Elizium,
To whose strait search I wholly me betook.

NOTES

'Song from the third eclogue'. The metre is based on 'poulter's measure', i.e. alternating lines of twelve and fourteen syllables.

2. Beta: Queen Elizabeth I.

30. After Ariadne's death Dionysius placed her wedding garland in the sky as a constellation (the Corona Borealis).

72. that foul seven-headed beast: the beast of the Apocalypse (*Revelation*, 13, 1), identified with the Church of Rome. In subsequent editions this line reads 'And Albion on the Apennines advance her conquering crest.'

'Ninth eclogue'. With this eclogue, cf. *Poly-Olbion*, Song 14, which describes a sheep-shearing feast in the Cotswolds, and Shakespeare, *The Winter's Tale*, IV, iv.

61. the widow's daughter of the glen: Rosalind, the beloved of Colin in Spenser's *The Shepheardes Calendar*, is so described in the *April* eclogue, line 26.

The Sonnets. Drayton's sonnets went through four recensions between 1594 and the final version of 1619. This selection is arranged chronologically to illustrate the various stages in their development.

Number 1.

1. Anker: Drayton's birthplace, Hartshill in North Warwickshire, stands above the river Anker, and Polesworth, the home of Anne Goodere ('Idea'), stands on the Anker a few miles lower down.

Number 5. This is a prefatory sonnet, addressed to the reader, which announces the changes made in 1599.

Number 6.

5-6. Jurors were required to view the body at an inquest.

Number 8.

10-11. Elliptical for 'False friends have . . .'

Number 14.

6-9. Robert Devereux, 19th Earl of Essex, born 1576, was executed for treason in 1601. The Irish rebel leader Hugh O'Neill, 3rd Earl of Tyrone (1550-1616) surrendered in 1603, in which year also Queen Elizabeth I died and King James I acceded to the throne. Peace with Spain was concluded on 19th August, 1604. The English people feared that the peace might entail a withdrawal of support from the Dutch, but in fact it did not.

Number 16. This sonnet is appropriately placed first in the 1619 sequence. The conceit of the voyage had been a commonplace since Petrarch, but Drayton's realistic navigational detail renews it.

8. the pole: the pole star.

'Endymion and Phoebe'.

5. Archelaus: 5th century B. C. philosopher, said to have taught Socrates.

31. The fir was associated with spears, but I have not found an association between Mars and the fir.

41-2. A reference to the legend of the golden apples guarded by a dragon and by the Hesperides ('daughters of the evening') in the Isles of the Blest or Fortunate Islands, supposed to be in the far west. The islands, and the garden, were also known as 'Hesperides'.

62. amaranthus: either an imaginary flower which never fades or love-lies-bleeding.

64. moly: a fabulous plant given to Odysseus to protect him from the sorceries of Circe.

'Rosamond to Henry'. Rosamond Clifford (d. 1176?), mistress of Henry II, was according to tradition hidden from Queen Eleanor's jealousy in a 'labyrinth' at Woodstock. There was in fact a group of buildings in the grounds of the palace which Henry was supposed to have built for Rosamond (see H. M. Colvin, *The History of the King's Works*, 1963). They stood round a spring which fed a series of fish ponds surrounded by cloistered courts, an arrangement which may have suggested a labyrinth.

40. The poem is set during the rebellion of 1173-4, in which Queen Eleanor joined with three of Henry's sons and the earls of Leicester, Chester, Derby and Norfolk against the king. In 1173 Henry was forty.

129-30. A reference to the inscription said to have been carved on Rosamond's tomb at Godstow nunnery near Oxford: 'Hic iacet in tumba Rosa mundi non rosa munda' ('Here lies in the tomb the fair but not the chaste rose of the world').

133-38. Rosamond's ancestors are mentioned in Domesday Book. Her father, brother, and brother-in-law gave gifts of land to Godstow for the repose of her soul, which suggests that they did not in fact cast her off.

155-8. Amymone, daughter of Danaus, was seduced by Neptune.

'Henry to Rosamond'.

37-8. Pope Alexander III threatened to excommunicate Henry unless he did penance for the murder of Thomas à Becket.

39. my rebellious son: Henry, 'the young king', who was crowned in his father's lifetime but died before him.

85-90. that great enchantress: Medea, who restored Aeson (the father of her lover, Jason) to youth by boiling him in a cauldron with magic herbs.

114. the guiltless: the 'wicked woman' mentioned by Rosamond ('The Epistle of Rosamond', lines 51-60).

154. A reference to Daniel's *The Complaint of Rosamond*, 1592.

180. Vaughan: William Warner's version of the story, in *Albion's England*, 1592, viii, 41, introduces a 'knight of trust' who guards Rosamond. In the ballad attributed to Thomas Deloney, one Sir Thomas plays a similar role. Drayton alone calls him Vaughan.

'The Barons' Wars'. This passage from the last canto of *The Barons' Wars* describes the arrest of Roger Mortimer at Nottingham Castle in October 1330. Mortimer (b. 1287) joined with the barons against Edward II and was imprisoned in the Tower. In 1324 he escaped to France (see l. 109), where he joined forces with Isabella, Edward's estranged queen. It was generally believed that he became her lover. His greed for power led to his arrest on a number of charges, including that of procuring the death of Edward II. He was executed in 1330.

25-40. Hyacinth was a youth loved by Phoebus Apollo, who killed him accidentally in a game of quoits (here, throwing the sledge, or hammer) and changed his blood into a flower.

46-8. Drayton refers to the kind of painting that can be seen in either of two ways, depending on the angle of vision.

49-50. Drayton's note reads 'Mercury feigned oft to court Hebe.'

122. Edward: Edward III. March: Mortimer was created 1st Earl of March in 1328.

171. their armour—the brightness, 1603. There is no equivalent in *Mortimeriados*, 1596. Cf. Spenser, *The Faerie Queene*, I, i, 14: 'His

glist'ring armour made/A little glooming light, much like a shade.'

189. In 1603 this line read 'Hate goes before, confusion followèd'. It has no equivalent in *Mortimeriados*.

273. youthful Neville and brave Turrington: Drayton's chief source here, John Stow's *Annals of England*, 1592, says that John Neville killed Hugh Turpington.

281. Skiddaw: a mountain in the centre of Cumberland.

The Odes.

'To Himself, and the Harp'.

81. Soowthern: John Soowthern published a collection of sonnets and odes (*Pandora*) in 1584, which borrowed heavily from Ronsard.

95. Skelton's rhyme: John Skelton (1460?-1529). His favourite verse-form is short-lined and irregular in rhyme and rhythm.

'An Ode Written in the Peak'. The Peak is a hilly district in NW Derbyshire. Drayton's knowledge of the place is also evident in *Poly-Olbion*, Song 26.

12. great Brutus: the legendary Trojan founder of London and ancestor of the British.

23. Camber: Wales. The name *Cambria* was thought to be derived from Camber, one of the three sons of Brutus, to whom was given the lands beyond the Severn.

'To the Virginian Voyage'.

1-6. The first successful expedition to colonize Virginia sailed in December 1606.

29. three harvests more: Drayton's information comes from *The Principal Navigations, Voyages, Traffiques and Discoveries of the English Nation*, 1598-1600, by Richard Hakluyt (1552?-1616) who is mentioned in line 68. Captain Barlowe's report of the first voyage to Virginia in 1584 says that 'their country corn . . . groweth three times in five months' (*Virginia Voyages from Hakluyt*, ed. D. B. and A. M. Quinn, 1973, p. 7).

36. sassafras: 'A kind of wood of most pleasant and sweet smell, and of most rare virtues in physic for the cure of many diseases' (Thomas Hariot's report, Quinn, p. 51).

37. to whom: the native population. (See Quinn, p. 8.)

'To the Cambro-Britons, and Their Harp, His Ballad of Agincourt'. Cambro-Britons: the Welsh. Harp: in the preface to the Odes, Drayton describes an ode as 'properly a song, moduled to the ancient harp.'

45. our grandsire: Edward III.

49. York: Edward, 2nd Duke of York, grandson of Edward III and the king's cousin, born 1373. He led the vanguard at Agincourt and was one of the two English peers killed there.

53. Exeter: Thomas Beaufort, 1st Earl of Dorset, created 2nd Duke of Exeter in 1416, d. 1426. He was the king's uncle. Holinshed and Shakespeare also say he was at Agincourt, but he was captain of Harfleur and may have remained there.

66. Erpingham: Sir Thomas Erpingham (1357-1428) ordered the English battle-line and gave the signal to attack.

68. our hid forces: two hundred bowmen in a low-lying meadow.

87. the French peasants: an insult.

95-6. The dented helmet is still in Westminster Abbey.

97. Gloucester: Humphrey of Lancaster, 2nd Duke of Gloucester, the king's brother, wounded at Agincourt. The king saved his life.

101. Clarence: Thomas of Lancaster, 2nd Duke of Clarence, the king's brother. Active at Harfleur, not certain if at Agincourt.

105. Warwick: Richard de Beauchamp, 13 Earl of Warwick and captain of Calais. Shakespeare too says he was at Agincourt, but the chroniclers do not.

106. Oxford: Richard de Vere, 11th Earl of Oxford (1385?-1417).

109. Suffolk: Michael de la Pole, 7th Earl of Suffolk, b. 1394?, killed at Agincourt.

110. Beaumont: Sir Charles de Beaumont. According to Hall and Holinshed, Beaumont, Willoughby and Fanhope were the commanders who led the vanguard together with the Duke of York. Willoughby: Robert de Willoughby, 6th Lord Willoughby.

112. Ferrers: Sir Edmund Ferrers, 6th Lord Ferrers of Chartley. Fanhope: Sir John Cornwall, created Baron of Fanhope in 1432.

'Poly-Olbion'. *Poly-Olbion*: a Greek word meaning 'rich in blessings', with a pun on *Albion*.

Song 6.

1-17. This passage describes the salmon-leap at Cenarth, NW Carmarthenshire.

Song 7.

1. The Wyre forest is in NW Worcestershire, near Bewdley.

3. the furnace: the introduction of the blast-furnace in the iron industry after about 1540 was a principal cause of the shortage of timber. Cf. *The Muses' Elizium*, the tenth nymphal, lines 29-32.

22. the son of Perops: Erysicthon was in fact the son of Triopas. Song 13. This passage is from Drayton's description of Warwickshire.

Song 23. This passage describes hare-coursing at Kelmarsh in N Northamptonshire.

2. Wat: short for Walter, a name for a hare.

16. wrench: to *wrench* is to turn the hare at less than a right angle. *OED* quotes the following: 'Sometimes the hare doth not turn, but wrench; for she is not properly said to turn, except she turn as it were round, and two wrenches stand for a turn' (1686).

Song 26.

4. Scarlock: Will Scarlet. George-a-Greene: the pinder of Wakefield who defeated Robin Hood and his companions. (A *pinder* is a pound-keeper and a *pound* is an enclosure for stray animals.)

'To ... Henry Reynolds'. Henry Reynolds: b. 1581, poet and author of *Mythomystes*, 1632, a critical essay on poetry.

19. *Pueriles*: probably the *Sententiae Pueriles*, a collection of Latin phrases. This and the *Disticha de Moribus* ('Moral Distichs') of Dionysius Cato (see line 20) were among the first texts studied in Elizabethan grammar-schools.

36. Mantuan: Johannes Baptista Spagnolo of Mantua (1448-1516), a writer of Latin eclogues used as a grammar-school text, as were Virgil's *Eclogues* (see line 37). These references show that Drayton received a grammar-school education. There is no reliable evidence that he ever studied at Oxford or Cambridge.

42. William Elderton: a ballad writer, d. 1592?

67. Bryan: Sir Francis Bryan, d. 1550. Almost all his poems are lost.

73. Gascoigne: George Gascoigne (1525?-1577), poet and playwright. Churchyard: Thomas Churchyard (1520?-1604) author of *Shore's Wife*, 1563, and *The Worthiness of Wales*, 1587.

97. Warner: William Warner (1558?-1609), author of *Albion's England*, 1586-1612, a metrical history of Britain.

151. Sylvester: Josuah Sylvester (1563-1618), translator of du Bartas (*Bartas, His Divine Weeks and Works*, 1605-8).

166. Alexander: Sir William Alexander of Menstrie, 1st Earl of

Stirling (1576?-1640), sonneteer and writer of tragedies.

171. Drummond: William Drummond of Hawthornden (1585-1649), poet and author of a *History of Scotland*, 1655.

175. the two Beaumonts: Sir John Beaumont (1583-1627), whose poem *The Metamorphosis of Tobacco*, 1602, has a dedicatory verse addressed to Drayton, and his brother Francis (1584-1616), the playwright. Browne: William Browne (1591-1643), author of *Brittania's Pastorals*, 1616, 1852, and the friend to whom Drayton's third *Elegy* is addressed.

185. post: title-pages of books were posted up as advertisements.

189. transcription: Drayton refers to the growing practice of circulating poems in manuscript and perhaps to Donne's poems in particular.

'Nymphidia'. The eight-line stanza (aaabcccb) of this poem is like the six-line 'tail-rhyme' (aabaab or aabccb) of Chaucer's *Tale of Sir Thopas*. The short lines are the tail, which in Drayton always ends with a feminine rhyme. *Nymphidia* (from the Greek word for 'bridal') is the name of the fairy from whom Drayton pretends to have the story of the poem.

1. Her chariot: that of the fairy queen (Mab, as in *Romeo and Juliet*). She has an assignation with her lover, Pigwiggen.

7. Fly Cranion: crane-fly (daddy-long-legs). Cf. *Romeo and Juliet*, I, iv, 65: 'Her waggoner, a small grey-coated gnat.'

65. the Tuscan poet: Ariosto, author of *Orlando Furioso*, 1532. Orlando (the Roland of the Charlemagne legend) was seized with a furious jealousy and ran naked through the countryside, destroying everything in his path.

68. Alcides: Hercules, who was driven mad by Juno and slew his wife and children (the subject of plays by Euripides and Seneca).

67. Ajax Telamon: the *Iliad* of Homer and the *Ajax* of Sophocles tell how Ajax, son of Telamon, slew a flock of sheep in his madness.

'Noah's Flood'.

33-6. The myth of the panther's sweet smell enticing other beasts to destruction comes from Pliny's *Natural History*, viii, 23.

71. Th'uneven-legged badger: it was commonly believed that the badger's legs were shorter on one side (usually thought to be the left,

according to Sir Thomas Browne) than the other.

'The Muses' Elizium'.

'The second nymphal'. Drayton defines *nymphal* (apparently his coinage) as 'a meeting or feast of nymphs'.

1. Lalus and Cleon are rival suitors for the hand of Lirope.

78. Lirope's 'father was a rivulet/Her mother was a fay.'

120. Tagus: a river in the Iberian Peninsula, famed for the gold supposed to be contained in its sands.

'The tenth nymphal'.

1. The nymphs have found an old satyr, a refugee from Felicia wandering in Elizium.

24. bid the base: to challenge, in the game called 'base' or 'prisoner's base'.

GLOSSARY

a-good: heartily

ambergris: a substance found in the intestines of the sperm-whale, used in perfumery

babian: baboon

baldric: belt worn over one shoulder and under the opposite arm

barley-break: an old country game

battening: thriving

bell-wether: the leading sheep of a flock, wearing a bell

bewray: betray, reveal

bilbo: sword from Bilbao in Spain, noted for the temper of its blade

breme: rough

browse: young shoots and twigs

butt: mark for archery practice

case, in: in condition

cassia: fragrant shrub or plant

chapelet: wreath for the head

cleve: cliff

clip: to kiss, embrace

clove of Paradise: a kind of clove-pink or carnation

clue: ball of thread

coil, what a: what a to-do

compass: angle of elevation (in archery)

corsive: n. corrosive

cote: n. cottage

cote: n. and vb. used of two dogs, in coursing, when one passes the other so as to give the hare a turn

counterpoyne: counterpane

cowslip of Jerusalem: lungwort

crankling: twisting

creek: winding passage
cut: cur
ding: to dash
dowset: doucet, a sweet dish
emmet: ant
estate: canopy
estridge: ostrich
flower-de-lice: fleur-de-lis, iris
forms herself: takes to her form
  (of a hare)
fret: ornament
frouncing: curling, frizzing
greave: thicket
gunning out: shooting out
haggard: untamed hawk
hecco: green woodpecker
hind: peasant
hoyle: a mark used when shoot-
  ing at 'rovers' (see *rove*)
humorous: moist
hunt's up: an early morning song
impresa: motto, maxim
jade: worn-out horse
Julyflower: gillyflower, clove-
  pink or wall-flower
kelled: webbed (from *kell*, a
  variant of *caul*)
letting: preventing
leven: lightning
libertine: one who goes his own
  way
limber: supple
loose: act of releasing an arrow
lustless: lacking in vigour
mavis: thrush
mell: to mingle, meddle
nervy: strong, sinewy
nice: careful

nope: bullfinch
orpharion: a kind of lute (from
  Orpheus and Arion)
ounce: lynx
ouzel: blackbird
owe: to own
peat: girl
penny-father: miser
pile: metal head of an arrow
pointed: appointed
preposterously: unnaturally
prick: n. target
prick: vb. to shoot at a 'prick'
qualm: swoon
quirister: chorister
ravin: prey
receipt: recipe
reed-sparrow: sedge warbler or
  reed bunting
revie: to retaliate
roundelay: song with a refrain
rove: to shoot without fixed aim
scathe: harm
scour: to drive away
shadow: vb. to paint or portray
  a likeness
silly: simple, innocent
simple: herb
sith: since
slade: valley, dell
smirking: smiling
spring: copse or wood of young
  trees
start-up: a kind of boot, laced
  above the ankle, worn by rustics
stover: winter food for cattle
strait: rigorous
swathe: broad track

tabret: small drum
taw: to tow
tedious: wearisome
thrill: to pierce
throstlecock: thrush
tire: head-dress
tralucent: translucent
twine: sb. twining stem or spray
  of a plant
tydie: a small bird, perhaps the
  goldcrest
ure: use

virelay: short-lined song
water-can: yellow water-lily
welked: of the welkin
whig: whey, sour milk or butter-
  milk
wilding: crab-apple or wild-apple
yellow-pate: yellowhammer
zany: mimic
zone: girdle